5-28-75

Buying
Home Furnishings

(Burlington House)

Patricia M. Williams

Buying Home Furnishings

ST. MARTIN'S PRESS
New York

St. Martin's Press
175 Fifth Avenue
New York, N.Y. 10010

1883728

FOR MY PARENTS
who furnished our home with love

Contents

Buying
Home Furnishings

ONE

Playing the Home Furnishings Game

Singles buy furniture. Newlyweds, too. When kids come along, more furniture is added as homes grow larger and needs change. Again, when kids grow up and move away and parents retrench, furniture is bought for that new stage of life. Furnishings must keep pace with the constant and changing demands of this lifetime cycle.

Home furnishings have been with us for a long, long time, and they've come a long way, baby. Carpets, furniture, lamps and accessories all serve practical functions, with the bonuses of comfort and beauty thrown in. The home furnishings you choose for your personal environment are tangible evidence of your personality and lifestyle . . . or what you wish your personality and lifestyle were. One of the all-time wise sayings of the industry is "People don't buy furniture: they buy dreams."

The single swinger, the bride-to-be, the rising young executive, the happy homemaker, the empty-nester—all have ideals of what their homes should be. Some choose furnishings to please themselves: some to please or impress others. Month after month women study slick magazines that depict the homes of the rich and famous, and dream that someday. . . . "Someday the kids will grow up and I'll get all-white

French Provincial for the living room." "Someday I'll get rid of Mom's hand-me-downs and buy all-new modern furniture." "Someday we'll panel and finish the basement and furnish it in Early American." Brides declare, "I know just what we want . . . as soon as we can afford it."

The bridal market is a big one, with brides and grooms annually pouring out $3.5 billion on home furnishings and appliances for their new homes. Almost 90 per cent of all new brides buy some furniture for their new homes—spending an average of $1,355—and 84.3 per cent of them buy it within six months of their weddings.

Of course, newlyweds aren't the only ones fueling the home furnishings industry. The Census Bureau reports that as of 1973 there were 12.6 million single-person households—with a big increase in men under 35 living alone in bachelor pads that need furniture.

Most single people live in apartments—another big market. The apartment and condominium business is booming. Some 21 million adults live in these dwellings, and statisticians delight in tallying their many home furnishings purchases. They often out-buy home-owners with equal incomes.

Both house and apartment dwellers are on the move. Sociologists point out that in the span of just one year one out of every five Americans— more than 40 million—will move from one residence to another. It is estimated that 55 per cent of all apartment dwellers will move within five years. Sociologists worry about the emotional and psychological strain of so much mobility, but the home furnishings industry knows that all that moving around means new carpets, furniture and accessories will be needed—probably over $1,000 worth per move.

Nearly three million American families have second homes—all demanding furnishings. Traditionally, mobile homes have been purchased fully furnished, but, to the delight of home furnishings merchants, it has been predicted that the bigger, more expensive, un-furnished mobile home will soon capture about 35 per cent of the total mobile-home market.

Even those who stay in one place buy furniture. The average American family with an established home spends $597 a year on home furnishings, according to figures for 1972 from the Bureau of Labor Statistics.

Every year Americans spend more on home furnishings than they did the year before, and the U.S. Department of Commerce expects that trend to survive inflations and recessions. With retail furniture sales topping $11 billion in 1974, the Department of Commerce projects retail sales to grow at a 7.5 per cent annual rate through 1980.

CONSUMING INTERESTS

Consumerism, women's lib and the youth movement—all have an impact on home furnishings retailers. Surveys are conducted one after another to compute the statistics and pinpoint the implications of these issues. Market meetings and panels are devoted to explanations and plans for coping with them. And yet things have not essentially changed.

Even though home furnishings are cited country-wide as a leading source of consumer complaints and dissatisfaction, consumerism is still damned and cursed at all levels within the industry—manufacturers, retailers and trade associations. Businesses of all kinds bitterly opposed the Truth-in-Lending law which was passed in 1969 (see Chapter 9). FTC regulations on labeling were fought hard before they were enacted, as were flammability standards for mattresses. Despite these defeats and despite warnings from within the industry ("Retailers and manufacturers must cooperate to establish effective consumer protection programs, or a third, less sympathetic party—the federal government—will do it for them."—National Home Furnishings Association's *Reports* magazine), consumer protection action is still strongly and almost indiscriminately opposed.

The Consumer Protection Agency bill—which was sponsored by Senators Charles Percy, Abraham Ribicoff, Jacob Javits, Warren Magnuson, Marlowe Cook and Frank Moss, and which was designed to monitor government agencies and intercede on the consumers' behalf—came under strong fire in mid-1974 and fell—for the time being—to frantic filibusters. The National Association of Manufacturers, the Chamber of Commerce of the United States, and the Grocery Manufacturers of America attacked the bill wildly, and Hampton Powell, the chairman of the Southern Furniture Manufacturers Association government relations committee, called it "one of the most dangerous pieces of legislation with which we have had to contend." The prevailing attitude remains one of head-in-the-sand resistance to the consumer movement.

WOMEN AND THE HOME FURNISHINGS INDUSTRY

The home furnishings consumer is a woman. Consumer studies sponsored by manufacturers and trade associations focus exclusively on women. Women under 30 and women over 30; working women and homemakers; blue-collar women, white-collar women and ring-around-the-collar women are all homogenized into computer print-outs. All categories are charted regarding frequency of purchase and motivation;

preferred stores and styles; hobbies and social life. Men simply do not enter into the picture—except in manufacturing, merchandising and selling. The industry—which deals in a commodity traditionally consigned to women—has few women executives, salespeople or decisionmakers.

What is surprising is the antiquated attitude of most home furnishings manufacturers and retailers toward women. Any with-it retailer knows that a hefty chunk of the nation's work force is female and that, according to a survey conducted for the Newspaper Advertising Bureau, Incorporated, in autumn of 1973, four out of ten married women between 18 and 30 are employed—and 91 per cent of those not working now have worked in the past and plan to work again. The retailer also knows that these statistics represent a lot of freedom, independence and disposable income—income that can be spent on home furnishings.

So far there's been a lot of talk given to these statistics and to women's changing role, but very little of that talk is reflected on the sales floor. In the face of women's increased spending power, educational level and independence, the home furnishings industry continues to see the woman shopper as emotional, indecisive, incompetent and childlike. Salesmen are encouraged to make shopping for home furnishings a pleasant, comforting experience for the woman by talking to her in vague but glowing terms of the many beauties and psychic benefits of her purchase. They are urged not to confuse her with talk of construction, materials, maintenance, warranties or finance plans.

Salesmen are advised to discuss the product with the woman, but to keep the husband handy to okay the price. Some stores even set up TV-watching, coffee-drinking lounges for the husbands so they can be lured to the store to approve the purchase. Nat Shore, senior vice president, E. T. Barwick Mills, instructed the Chicago Floor Covering Association members that "The good salesman listens, finds out what the customer's needs and wants are. After all, it's her money!" O.K., it's *her* money. Then why this follow-up on clinching the sale: "Seek out something extra—and I'll tell you, that is always the old man. Get Daddy on your side—she's been working on him for three years to say yes to new carpet, and if he says, 'We're buying from Irving here,' you think she's gonna say no?"

While most couples do make major furniture purchases a joint decision, the retailer too often translates this fact into treating the woman to a series of "Isn't this a nice color?", "Can't you just see this in your living room?", "This style just seems to suit your personality," while the husband gets the hard facts and credit data. As the consumer of the home furnishings industry, woman deserves better.

THE PEPSI GENERATION

Although there are organized consumer groups and women's-interest groups, the youth group per se is not organized. It is simply a large and often misunderstood buying power. Again, like women, young people are tabulated to the last decimal point by market research firms—with good reason. Management Horizons, Incorporated, research indicates that the Pepsi generation's 24- to 35-year-olds are the front-runners in terms of consumer demand. They will account for the largest share of U.S. spending power in the seventies, some 26 per cent of all before-tax income. In 1970 there were about 15 million families headed by persons under 35; by 1980 the number will exceed 23 million. Department of Commerce figures show that in 1970 28 per cent of all homes in the 24-34 age bracket had incomes of $10,000 or over. No matter how you chart it, the youth market is impressively powerful.

What furnishings are consistently promoted for the youth market? Plastic furniture, assemble-it-yourself furniture, beanbags, oversized pillows, inflatables, paper furniture, op, pop, mod vinyl fabrics. Why? Well, young people, single or married, are receptive to new ideas and materials, and individually they don't have a lot of money—so they are offered cheap, faddish junk. But is that what they want? For a pick-up-and-go lifestyle, maybe; for setting up a home, no. *Seventeen* magazine found that quality furniture tops the list of essentials that teen-age brides want in their homes—and half of them want that furniture right away. Sixty per cent of the respondents to *Seventeen's* questionnaire want original art in their homes, and 54 per cent plan to purchase authentic antiques. Doesn't sound like the plastic generation, does it?

Retailers who cater to young people recognize the desire for instant gratification. They staff the sales floors with young people and have instant availability of most home furnishings items. No wait for shipment, no wait for delivery. Do it yourself. These stores also make dealing in plastic money—credit cards—easy, quick and painless.

Not only do young people want quality, but they also have expressed in no uncertain terms an interest in returning to natural things, in the environment, in functionalism—in a need to get back to the basics. But, of course, mass production does not lend itself to naturalness. When the simplicity of the natural-wood butcher block scored heavily with young people, manufacturers responded with vinyl-wrap butcher-block prints over particle board. The denim look went over big, so the home furnishings market was glutted with denim-look vinyl, high-pressure laminate denim—even television sets covered in denim. With the advent of the conservation movement, plastic animal horns were introduced for the ecology buffs. Somehow the industry seemed to miss the point.

Young people are acutely aware of the rip-off by big business. They are very skeptical of the trustworthiness of retailers in general and specifically distrust most salesmen. As consumers they see that the battle lines are clearly drawn.

THE ONLY GAME IN TOWN

At the most basic level the home furnishings industry operates like any other industry. The manufacturer produces a product which he sells to the retailer, who, in turn, sells it to the consumer. As in other industries, success depends on the nation's economic situation. If a housing boom fizzles, the fizzle is felt in home furnishings about 12 months later, according to the research and accounting firm Seidman & Seidman. If personal income climbs, furniture shipments will climb three months later; if consumers feel depressed about the economy, furniture shipments will be depressed about four months later.

The home furnishings industry is like no other. It is massive, moving more than $11 billion worth of home furnishings into the nation's homes every year, and extremely diverse, with all kinds of products—furniture, carpeting, bedding, lamps and accessories—in countless styles and at all conceivable quality levels. Also, the home furnishings industry is fragmented by fierce infighting. Manufacturers are more concerned with beating out one another than with giving consumers what they need and want.

Some observers believe it is that very competitiveness that has resulted in the industry's system of devising constant style changes with which to bedazzle retailers. Other, more cynical observers see the quick changes as simple evidence of forced obsolescence. In *U.S. News & World Report's* 1974 book *How to Live with Inflation*, it is flatly stated that "Unfortunately, in recent years manufacturers have sought to create fashion obsolescence in furniture to try to keep their share of a market declining in the face of strong fashion merchandising by the apparel and car industries. One example is the 'mod' look in furniture, featuring splashy colors like the mod look in clothing."

The frequent introduction of new furniture fashions results in mediocre designs, adds to the consumer's cost, worsens the factory delivery problem, and even makes it difficult to purchase matching furniture at a later date, as styles are discontinued.

TO MARKET, TO MARKET

These controversial style changes are introduced at giant biannual home furnishings markets. Markets are held—not simultaneously—in several cities, and manufacturers, retailers, buyers, salesmen, designers, suppliers and press people come flooding in for a frantic two or three days of meetings, conferences, shopping, partying and dealing.

Markets are held in market buildings. Seems reasonable enough, right? Not altogether. These market buildings are huge, ever-expanding or ever-modernizing structures in the expensive downtown areas, and manufacturers rent showrooms in them. Some of these showrooms are open daily to the trade, but many are open only one day a week—again, only to the trade. Still others are open only during markets—about two weeks out of the year. That's right. A manufacturer rents a showroom for 12 months and uses it only two weeks a year!

Joe Cappo, the Chicago *Daily News* marketing columnist, says, "The function of a marketing man in most businesses is to make it easier for a customer to buy. In the furniture industry, the so-called marketing men seem to be daring the customer to buy." He sees the closed showroom as part of the industry's "un-marketing strategy."

Thousands of home furnishings items are presented in miles of exciting and colorful showrooms—and the consumer is denied access to them without a retailer or interior designer as chaperon. Some market buildings, for a slight fee, have begun to offer consumers limited tours of a few spaces, but building managers say that opening the buildings to the public would be too costly in terms of security, insurance and other services. In the autumn of 1974 the New York Furniture Exchange instituted a policy of permitting consumers to tour the exchange when accompanied by a registered, vetted, security-checked retailer. A storm of protests and legal action from tenant-exhibitors followed. They didn't want to talk price in front of consumers; many simply adopted their own "closed-door" policy. Retailers feared that manufacturers would sell direct to the consumer; others worried that non-bona fide retailers would gain admittance. Whatever the reasons given, consumers are not welcome at market buildings. They are missing a good bet. Even those only slightly interested in home furnishings cannot fail to be impressed by the stunning panorama of products, styles, and displays filling the enormous structures. Furnishings are presented as the designer conceived them: in full room groupings totally coordinated and accessorized for the best possible effect. Following a tour of market showrooms, one woman described the experience as "nothing like being in a store."

THE DREAM MERCHANTS

Although the direct manufacturer-to-retailer pipeline is the one most often used in home furnishings, some segments of the industry put wholesalers in the middle. Carpeting is often sold to retailers through wholesale distributors, and wholesale showrooms are often set up to service interior designers. Interior designers may also buy direct from manufacturers to sell to the consumer. More about them in Chapter 5.

Home furnishings are sold to the consumer through a wide variety of retail outlets—full-service stores, warehouse-showrooms, specialty stores, discount operations and department stores. The furniture industry is peculiar in that the major burden of promotion and advertising to the consumer falls on the retailer. More than on anything else— service, style or brand names—the retailer tends to concentrate on the price in his ads.

How does the pricing system work? Typically, if a retailer buys an item from the manufacturer for, say, $100, he marks it up to sell at retail for $200. This is called working on a "number." Some stores operate at "number plus 10, 20, or 30." That is, the mark-up plus 10, 20 or 30 per cent. Under this system, the retail price escalates from $200 to as much as $230.

If this information tempts you to start ranting about price-gouging and overpricing, you should remember that furniture demands a higher markup than most other goods, because of the costs involved. The home furnishings retailer operates on a slow rate of stock turnover and must pay freight charges, inspect and, if necessary, repair damaged goods on arrival. He has to maintain a warehouse, showroom, trucks; pay salaries of sales staff, office personnel, delivery crew and decorators, as well as pay operating costs and advertising expenses. After all that, the markup is clearly not sheer profit. Most of the number-plus-percentage stores claim they must add the percentage markup because of higher operating costs.

Don't begrudge the markup—as long as it is a fair one. Watch out for the overblown markup. As J. Paul Getty, the world's richest man, says, "I pay the going rate, but I don't see any reason for paying more than you have to." Words to live by.

KEEP YOUR OPTIONS OPEN

What alternatives do you have to paying the price and dealing with the system? Well, you can buy used furniture and antiques. Some people contend that old furniture is stronger and better made than the furniture of today, and probably some of it is—but not all. There is junk furniture today, and there was junk furniture yesterday. Simple age doesn't make it better. Refinishing needed on much old furniture, when done by a competent craftsman, can run up the cost of that bargain quicker than you can say "Ralph Nader." Refinishing done by you is economical only if you do a good job.

If you're into antiques, you know you're paying for the very fact that the piece is an antique. That piece may not be durable, sturdy or attractive. The antique shopper is not looking for the same qualities as the home furnishings shopper.

You can follow the suggestions in the women's magazines and craft books and "decorate on a budget," using "more wit than money." Lamps made from bleach bottles, bookcases converted from orange crates, curtains fashioned from macaroni and paper cups—somehow, under the strain of daily living and in harsh sunlight and the even harsher glare of a mother-in-law's eye, few of these ideas really succeed.

It's a mistake to buy or make something just because it's inexpensive. In June 1973 *Glamour* ran a feature called "1/2/3, and an Empty Apartment Turns Into Your Place." The article, aimed at those furnishing a first apartment on a "really tight budget," suggested making a sofa from "three sausage-shaped pieces stuffed with shredded foam and belted together." Don't fall prey to such budget-extenders. For this one you would have to buy shredded foam and fabric, and, after struggling to stuff the fabric tubes, you would have three foam-rubber sausages—not a sofa. In fact, the sausages don't provide seating for anyone other than an acrobat or a child. The money this project requires could be saved for a real sofa or could buy some large floor cushions that would provide immediate, inexpensive seating and, later, serve as colorful accessories.

Unfinished furniture is another do-it-yourself idea. Good unfinished furniture can cost as much as cheap finished furniture, but, as Martin Porris, a consumer advocate, says, "Buying do-it-yourself furniture can save you money and help create a warm and glowing relationship between you and your home environment." Right—but if you don't know what you're doing in assembling, sanding and finishing, that "warm and glowing relationship" can become a heated one as you end up with furnishings that look like the leftovers from a fire sale.

Recycled furniture will take you a step ahead of the herd in terms of both ecological awareness and creativity. Nobel laureate Glenn T. Seaborg has predicted that the nation will become "a recycle society by the 1990's." Furniture is running ahead of this schedule and is already available in recycled materials that can be folded up on a moment's notice to suit a nomadic existence. Although much of this recycled cardboard furniture is quite simple and utilitarian, of the fold-and-slot variety and in the cheap-to-inexpensive bracket, one manufacturer has already turned out recycled-paper occasional furniture with a mar-resistant finish, the feel of suede and a stiff price tag. A silicon-based coating reportedly offers some degree of fire and water resistance to cardboard furniture.

However, for most people these alternatives aren't valid. They don't want living rooms filled with craft projects, Salvation Army bargains and cardboard. They want new, honest-to-God furniture. Furniture that will endure to give comfort, service and beauty for many years. Furniture that will help to turn an apartment or house into a home.

Some accessories aside, home furnishings are big-ticket purchases. That is, the price on the sales ticket is a big one. Many different kinds of stores sell home furnishings—some reputable, some not. There are all kinds of styles, materials and colors to choose from—some good, some not. Some items are well made and will give years of service; others are badly made and will fall apart in no time. Display tricks, pricing gimmicks, misleading ads, smooth sales talks are landmines in the home furnishings showroom. Finance charges can turn a fair price into an outrageous one. All of this is true, but you need not be intimidated. With a little preparation, buying home furnishings can be a satisfying experience.

The government and consumer action groups are working to protect you in the marketplace, but they're not omnipresent and you as a consumer have an obligation to inform yourself. Do your homework. Learn what different kinds of stores offer. Know what price, style and color you want before you go to the store. Know what you expect of the item you are considering buying. There is no need to become an expert in all areas of home furnishings, but you should know enough to be able to ask intelligent questions and evaluate the answers.

Time invested in learning how to buy home furnishings will save you both time and money as you shop. You will be justifiably confident—and, who knows, you might even enjoy yourself.

TWO

Name Your Price

Furniture buying involves a fair amount of decision making, long-range planning and dollar spending, but it has its fun side too. You get to flop onto squooshy chairs; stretch out on rolling, gurgling water mattresses; and exclaim, "Who would ever buy that?!" and "Ohhh, isn't that gorgeous!" You can prowl through stores, flip through home furnishings magazines, collect swatches and color samples—turn it into a season-long project, if you wish. BUT—before the fun begins, you must do some financial figuring, and after the fun you must pay for your purchases. It's like a sandwich: money planning, fun buying, money paying. If you do it right, that sandwich should not be too hard to swallow.

You must learn to view your furniture as an investment. Explaining why young people are willing to spend as much as $2,000 for a Baker four-poster bed, Frank Van Steenberg, chairman of Baker Furniture Company, Incorporated, manufacturer of fine-quality furniture, said, "Like good china and silver, it is an investment for a lifetime. It will never be obsolete."

Although relatively few young couples pay $2,000 for a bed, most home furnishings purchases are major expenditures that should be carefully considered and should pay off in years of service. Just one item— say, a sofa—is going to cost anywhere from a minimum of a couple of hundred dollars to a possible sum in the thousands.

Obviously, furniture is not cheap. In fact, cheap furniture usually

11

turns out to be most expensive, as it gives poor service in return for dollars spent. Carefully chosen furniture can, however, be a very good investment. Richard E. Burow, president of Kroehler Manufacturing Company, one of the nation's largest furniture manufacturers, recently said, "I did a little checking on one of our own sofas and discovered that a $280 model costs the shopper only $1.65 a pound. . . . For the family who use a sofa for ten years, the cost is still less per day than the price of an evening newspaper."

This technique of minimizing cost by expressing it in terms of years of service is a common gambit used to induce the consumer to spend more initially. In a sales-training booklet, Stanley Furniture Company advises retail salespeople, "As a budgeteer [*sic*] it is your responsibility to 'simplify' for your customer the expenditure of an additional $100, $500 or whatever the amount may be." The salesperson is instructed to use a chart to dramatize how an investment in furniture can be amortized over the years.

Good furniture is a good investment, but don't spend $100 or $500 more than you planned just because it's going to average out to pennies a day in ten years. You're going to pay for it *now*.

THE BUDGET—WHY AND HOW

Don't start pumping your dream machine full of investment-worthy shag carpets, eight-foot sofas, triple dressers and chrome étagères until you make a budget. When you're anxious to get out into the showrooms and start selecting furniture, budget-making can seem a bore, but buying without a financial plan can be the direct route to disaster.

True enough, home furnishings can add comfort and beauty to your home. Unplanned purchases of home furnishings can also add massive debt and accompanying arguments. Thomas A. Harris, the transactional analyst of "I'm O.K.—You're O.K." fame, estimates that 70 to 80 per cent of those who come to his institute for help are in financial difficulties. He believes that, in most cases, these difficulties are caused by lack of planning. Many family counselors have found that disagreements over money cause the greatest number of marital problems.

Essentially, your plan should come down to: how much have you got to spend and what should you spend it on? If you have savings that you wish to spend on home furnishings, your first question is easily answered. If not, money will have to come from your monthly income, and this should be budgeted.

First, list the absolute necessities—food, clothing, shelter, health allotments, etc. Deduct these from your income and decide how much of the balance you wish to spend on furnishing your home. You may then save that amount monthly until you have enough to make a purchase, or you may use this sum monthly for installment payments. If you choose to go the time-payment route, you must consider the extra costs involved (see Chapter 9).

Next, list the pieces of furniture you need. If you are establishing your first home or apartment, you will, of course, have a long list.

Home ec. teachers are often fond of parceling budgets out in room-by-room percentages, as: living room, 35 per cent of budget; dining room, 25 per cent; bedroom, 20 per cent; family room, 10 per cent; kids' room, 10 per cent. However, such arbitrary percentages are meaningless to all but the teacher. Your personal needs and desires—your lifestyle—should determine how much you choose to spend on what. If you wish to entertain often and impressively, you may be willing to spend as much as 70 per cent of your home furnishings budget on the living room and dining room. Or you may share your home with only one other person and do that sharing mainly in a fantasy-style bedroom outfitted with a custom-made bed—round, revolving and mirrored—covered with sensuous, expensive fabric and heaped with fur pillows. If that's where your interests lie, spend your money there—but do it on a budget.

Funds may be allocated another way too. There are certain items of furniture that you can scrimp on and others that really should be the best you can afford. Casegoods, for example—tables, dressers, cabinets, etc.—should be purchased for real staying power. It is casegoods that most often get passed along as family heirlooms or turn up in antique shops. Doesn't an older couple you know have their original bedroom set while sitting on their fourth or fifth sofa? A reasonably good dresser or chest will endure for as long as you wish it to, with a minimum of care. Unless you are given to dancing on your dining room table in moments of excitement, the table should survive years of more traditional banquets.

Accessories, of course, can be real budget-stretchers. Even without going all artsy-craftsy and making wall hangings from old margarine tubs, you can save by finding well-designed accessories—lamps, wall décor, planters, etc.—at modest prices. Certainly museum prints in Plexiglas frames are bargains; but even supermarket promotions can turn up some acceptable works of "art."

Even the most enthusiastic and resourceful installment-plan shopper will find it difficult to buy everything at one time. If you are on a tight budget, you must determine what pieces are absolutely essential. Bedding, a dining table and chairs, and seating—probably a sofa and an upholstered chair—are the usual basics. A storage piece or two will likely also be needed, and most people would add a TV. A word of warning: if you will probably be moving within a year or so—and probably thereafter again and again—keep such probabilities in mind when choosing furniture. Keep it portable. Don't buy a nine-foot sofa, a massive breakfront or a king-sized bed. Avoid anything that will be awkward to move or will make size demands that not all apartments or houses can answer.

According to a survey by *Bride's* magazine, most newlyweds spend a good chunk of their respective budgets on bedroom furniture. That's rather endearing and romantic, but romance need not overwhelm the budget. Too often young couples spend thousands on enormous, multipiece bedroom sets even before they have chosen apartments.

Terry and Fran were graduating from college in June and getting married in July. Terry's parents generously gave the kids $1,500 earmarked for buying home furnishings. Without an apartment or house even in mind, let alone rented, the about-to-be-marrieds went shopping and bought a $1,500 bedroom set. The set had a king-sized bed, a triple dresser, two oversized nightstands and a massive chest. Now, when they go apartment hunting, they must find an apartment with a reasonable rent, in a good neighborhood, near shopping and transportation—and with a bedroom the size of a modest ballroom. Of course, they don't have to worry about the sizes of the rest of the apartment's rooms; they have no money with which to furnish them.

Although we have been trained to think of bedroom furniture in terms of sets, there is no need whatever to start out with a set. If money is scarce, buy a good mattress and foundation and put them on a metal frame.

This same idea can be applied to any room. When working on a restricted budget, you will do better to buy pieces one at a time. Buy a good mattress instead of a poor-quality bedroom set; buy a good-quality sofa instead of an inferior living room set. One good piece that will last for years, give good service and add to the beauty of your home is a better investment than an entire houseful of junk.

The one-thing-at-a-time approach also allows for some creative thinking along the way. You get to live with what you have chosen and develop new ideas or reinforce the old.

Multipurpose furniture is a good budget-extender. The sleeper sofa, for example, serves two purposes for the price of one. Extendible or foldable tables that double as desks, game tables that can double as dining tables, indoor-outdoor director's chairs, bookcases that work as room dividers—all help extend tight money and can later, when funds are flush, serve a gracious single purpose.

Watching and waiting for sales is another smart way to save money. That table you like so well but just can't quite afford may well come into reach during a good sale. A word of warning: when shopping during sales, watch out for damaged or otherwise-imperfect items. Check and double-check for scratches, mars, dents, tears, discolorations, and other flaws. On many sales you have no return or refund privileges, so you had better make sure the color is what you want and the piece is in perfect condition.

Traditionally, seasonal furniture sales are held in February and August. Of course, there are many promotions offered throughout the year: anniversary sales, private sales, one-day sales, special-purchase sales and holiday sales of all kinds. The National Retail Merchants Association offers a "Bargain Calendar" listing the months of the year when stores usually offer best buys. The calendar cites June and August for bedding specials; January and June for floor coverings; January, June, July, August and October for furniture; and January, May and October for other home furnishings items such as lamps, wall décor, etc.

Don't be swayed into impulse buying by bargain prices. If you have low-watt will power, stay away from hysterical "moment of madness" sales where bells ring and sirens wail to announce short-duration (15- to 30-minute) sales. You've made a budget—stick to it.

A survey of 308 shoppers indicated that 112 of them waited until they were actually in the store before shaping their ideas about purchases. Another survey of nearly 7,000 shoppers showed that fully half of all impulse purchases were made simply because the impetuous shopper saw it displayed and wanted it.

As the charge-account concept has grown, purchase planning has diminished. In 1945 only 40.8 per cent of purchases were unplanned: by 1965 56.8 per cent were unplanned, and that figure has grown over the years that have followed.

Spur-of-the-moment decisions to spend several hundred dollars can be regretted for months to come. If you don't need it, if it doesn't fit into your decorating scheme, if it's not in the budget, it's a loser. Impulse buying leads to mismatched rooms and overburdened budgets.

RENT NOW, OWN IT NEVER

If you must move frequently, renting furniture may save you money; but there are many pitfalls in renting. Costs often vary with the style of furniture chosen: contemporary is usually less expensive than, say, French Provincial. Take a hard look at the total *annual* rental costs: check out delivery and pickup charges, find out who is responsible for maintenance and repairs. The simple monthly fee may not be great, but it is possible to pay out as much rent over a two-or three-year period as you would spend to furnish a home or apartment . . . and since you can't sell what you don't own, you can't recover any of this expense when you must move.

DO YOU SAVE BY REUPHOLSTERING WHAT YOU HAVE?

Confronted with worn furniture and limited budgets, shoppers often desperately cast about for an alternative to buying costly new furniture. Inevitably they turn to considering reupholstery or slipcovers. If you are thinking of having a sofa or chair reupholstered, do some comparison shopping first. Check out the cost of the reupholstering against the cost of a *similar* new item. The upholstery fabric is generally only a small part of the total cost; reupholstery is strictly custom work, and the labor costs pile up quickly. Of course, a good firm will essentially rebuild the furniture. They replace the filling materials, tie the springs, strengthen the frame and replace the cover. Without doubt, the life of the piece is extended by many years. However, unless the furniture was very fine, an heirloom or of great sentimental value, you will probably wind up spending much more than it was worth. Most moderately-priced furniture is not worth reupholstery costs.

Slipcovers will, of course, cover threadbare upholstery, but they do nothing for worn construction. At best, slipcovers can postpone the purchase of new furniture, but it should be remembered that they are only a *temporary* solution. Their cost, then, should be kept low.

HOW GOOD IS GOOD ENOUGH?

What do you have to spend to get a good sofa? Mattress? Table? We've all heard, "You get what you pay for" and "You can't get something for nothing." True enough—you can't get something for nothing. But price alone is not a guarantee of quality. Retailers often price an item well above its "suggested retail price" if it "looks like more." For example, if standard pricing would indicate that a chair wholesaling for $38.50 should sell for $69.95, but that chair looks like a $90 chair, then it's not unlikely that $90 it will be. You didn't get a better chair—the retailer just made a better profit.

In the summer of 1973 a manufacturer offered a living room group—a sofa and two chairs—to retail at $299. That same group was later featured "ON SALE"—at "the greatest sale of the year" no less—at an Illinois chain for $699. "Regular $799.99 value." In letters one-inch high, shoppers were urged to "SAVE $100." On what—a set that is priced $400 over the manufacturer's suggested retail price?

If a store owner is paying high rent or is loaded with extra services, you are probably going to pay more than you would to a dealer with a lower overhead or higher volume.

No, the customer doesn't always get what he or she pays for.

Beating this all-the-traffic-will-bear pricing gimmick is not easy. It helps to shop at a reliable dealer who is interested in repeat business, to inform yourself about "going" prices and to learn how to detect furniture quality.

The Home Furnishings Council, a now-defunct industry-sponsored organization, published a booklet called *Consumer-Buying Facts on Home Furnishings*. In this booklet the question "How much do you have to pay to get a sofa that will hold up with an active family?" is answered, "It is possible to buy sofas which will provide good service for less than $300. At this price you are able to buy a well-constructed wood frame, proper springs, good comfort and a durable fabric. Ask the salesman to help you recognize a good value." How's that for meaningless? How much is less than $300? Five bucks or $299? And "ask the salesman to help you recognize a good value"—uh huh, that's like a sheep asking a wolf to help him find a good hiding spot.

To answer the "How much do I have to spend" question, let's compare a furniture purchase to buying a car. When you decide to buy a car, you go out and shop around, compare the market. Pretty soon you have an idea of what you have to spend for basic, reliable transportation. Anything below that is suspect, right? ("I can sell you this little baby for $1,500—of course, if you want the seats, that's extra.") Anything above that basic price is an option or luxury extra. You may be able to buy a pared-down minicompact that will give good service at quite a low price, but you may not find it satisfactory. You may want a heavy car, or more elbow room or bigger trunk space or even just a more impressive car. Options such as air conditioning, radio, tinted windshield all drive the price up. So it is with furniture.

A quick survey of the market will show you the price spread—from low to medium to high—in your area. Because of regional variations, industry price changes and the fluctuations of the national economy, it is not possible here to list low, medium and high prices in dollars and cents. It should soon become clear that to obtain essential good-construction features you will have to pay a certain price, and that over that price you are paying for options, such as quilted fabric, a hand-rubbed finish. The Home Furnishings Council's booklet takes a turn for the better and offers the following sensible information: "There can be as much [as] or more than $200 difference in similar-appearing sofas. The difference is in the construction and the fabric. For example, one traditional sofa may have a simple, yet sturdy coil-spring base, good hardwood frame, resilient polyurethane seat cushions and an attractive, durable fabric, and be priced at $300. Next to it at $500 may be another traditional sofa, with double-cone coil springs; cushions filled with down, foam padding to soften the arms; casters and a decorative, expensive matching fabric cover. In terms of service it might not last any longer, but it would give the purchaser the feeling of owning a more luxurious sofa. The choice should be determined by the need and the budget.

"Price does not always dictate quality . . . often it indicates luxury features. It might even represent the difference between an advertised and nonadvertised brand."

WHAT ABOUT BRAND NAMES?

Lord Peter Wimsey, the aristocratic sleuth in Dorothy Sayers' well-known mystery novels, was right again when he said in *Murder Must Advertise*, "One does not . . . consider the brand to be the guarantee of quality. For us, the quality guarantees the brand."

Despite such industry hokum as "Brand-Name Retailer" awards, the fact that a furniture brand is well known only guarantees that the manufacturer has invested a considerable sum in advertising. That may be because he is proud of the product and will stand behind it—or it may not.

Most of us view breakfast-food and cosmetic advertising with a somewhat cynical eye. We have no good reason to be any more trusting about furniture brand advertising.

However, some manufacturers do consistently produce quality furniture and give the consumer a good return for every dollar spent. If you have enjoyed a manufacturer's product, by all means remember his name and shop for that brand. In this way brand names can be watched for and used as quality indicators.

It also pays to go the the library and read through several weeks' worth of *Home Furnishings Daily*, the home furnishings paper for the trade. In it you will find manufacturers advertising themselves as "low-end" or "promotional." You will get a fair indication of mid-price and top-quality brands—plus a few inside tips.

If a known brand is not necessarily good, what does that say about an unknown private label? Often a very large dealer will have a private-label line made just for him. Some so-called consumer advocates recommend the private brand as giving more value for less money because "it doesn't share the cost of expensive advertising and packaging." That may be true in some cases, but it is also true that while private-label goods may share the factory with brand-name goods, they need not be made to the same specifications. A manufacturer of upholstered goods, for example, may produce just the quality ordered—medium to low. He may back his own line with wear guarantees, but he doesn't back the private label. It is up to the dealer to do that.

REGIONAL SNOBBERY

The geographic area of a manufacturer has no bearing on quality, either. In his book *More for Your Money* (Chemical Publishing, 1970) H. Bennett contends that furniture made in Grand Rapids, Michigan, is tops and that "Because of the demand for low-priced furniture many factories have sprung up in the South and other sections, which turn out cheaper grades. These fill a legitimate need. Unfortunately, some of this production is sold at inflated prices and represented as high-quality furniture." That is utter rubbish. Some of the finest furniture in the country is made in the South and, in fact, High Point, North Carolina, has grown to be the furniture-manufacturing capital of the United States, producing furniture at all price and quality levels. Factories in and around High Point produce 60 per cent of the bedroom furniture, 52 per cent of the dining room furniture and 28 per cent of the upholstered furniture made in this country. There is no validity whatever in determining furniture quality on the basis of the geographic area in which it is manufactured.

YOU ARE YOUR FURNITURE

The industry devotes much effort to convincing women that their value as wives, mothers and homemakers is inextricably bound up with the furnishings in their homes. A decorator speaking to a high school home economics class explains seriously, "The largest part of your life is spent at home. The character of your children will be molded, in part, by the lifestyle of your home. Your marriage may stand or fall on your success or failure as a couple to establish a happy home." She goes on to urge the students to seek trained professional help in "making your first house truly a home."

In the spirit that made Hallmark great, home decorating magazines gush, "Homes are the heartbeat of America," "Home is where the heart is," "Home is the center of a woman's universe," "Her home is a reflection of the woman."

In Celanese's *Room Service*—a promotional booklet designed to "introduce you to an exciting modern concept, help you develop a new point of view, a new dimension for yourself, your family, AND YOUR HOME!"—young families are urged to create a "family-formal" library in lieu of the ordinary recreation room. The book-walled room illustrated features a crystal chandelier, white armchairs and sofa, and shag carpeting. The average bunch of kids would reduce it to a shambles after one Saturday afternoon, you say? Ah no, Celanese coos, "Actually children are not more careless, more destructive or more indifferent to their surroundings than adults. The highly normal, highly active youngsters in this family *love* the library . . . They warm to its hospitality . . . And if the child-study experts are right, they are *highly* influenced by a serene, beautiful atmosphere." It sounds great—but before you shell out for a family-library, make sure it rings true for your family's way of life. Maybe your kids would rather warm to a mom and dad who aren't worried about how to pay for that crystal chandelier. Maybe you would all be happier poking a broken spring back into the sofa while getting back in the black.

Your kids won't love you more because your sofa is new. You can't bridge the infamous generation gap with shag carpeting. Children do appreciate having a nice home to which they can bring their friends; however, a nice home can be clean, neat and happy without being a decorator's delight. A wandering spouse will not be lured home by new slipcovers.

When parceling out your budget and debating whether or not you can afford $900 for a new family room grouping, ask yourself whether or not your family room would be a happier place if the money were spent on something other than furniture—or perhaps not spent at all. Don't get caught up in the status game. Don't fall prey to the lure of *House Beautiful*. Marriages are not made secure by beautifully furnished homes, but they can certainly be made insecure by strained financial situations. Spend your money wisely; spend it on a budget—and sometimes, spend it not at all.

THREE

Fads vs. Classics– in Color

Taste, like beauty, is in the eye of the beholder. What is *good* taste? Who knows? *Vogue* and *House Beautiful* repeatedly run features in which tastemakers of the day attempt to define their concepts of good taste. Even within the magazines' narrow limits of fashion and the times, social background and wealth, there is no general agreement.

The *American Heritage Dictionary* defines taste as both "the faculty of discerning what is aesthetically excellent or appropriate" and "a personal preference or liking for something." Unfortunately, there are no set guidelines to follow for finding a chair that is "aesthetically excellent." A spare, straight-lined Shaker chair and a baroque, massive Louis XIV chair may both be considered in good taste, and they are as unlike as possible. You can't walk into a furniture store with a handy checklist of aesthetic qualities: harmonious line, balanced design, rich colors. "Yes, this chair has two out of three of the most wanted aesthetic qualities. I'll take it."

So you turn to interior decoration books and find page after page of vague, adjective-loaded talk of harmony, balance, rhythm and emphasis summed up with a quote such as, "Good design attracts and pleases the eye; bad design repels it." Right, no arguing about that, except . . . what pleases my eye may not please yours and certainly may not get the "Good-Taste Seal of Approval."

But that does bring us to the concept of "pleasing." Your eye should, indeed, be pleased by the furniture you choose to live with. If your personal taste pleases you and your family, then, within that framework, it is good. If you are able to say with honesty, "I don't care what anybody else thinks is good taste. I know my own preferences and that's what I want"—O.K. You're secure and will pick and choose with confidence.

Not everyone can make that statement. Charles Stendig, owner of Stendig, Incorporated, a firm specializing in avant-garde furnishings, says, "The problem is, furnishings seem to necessitate some sort of approval that people need from friends or neighbors.

"Nobody worries about a neighbor's reaction to a new name-brand refrigerator. But when it comes to furniture—it's all out there in the open. You can see the sofa. Touch the chair. And some big hang-up occurs if a friend doesn't like it.

"That's not the point of furniture," Stendig contends. "Furniture should create an excitement. Like, when I was a kid, I had a cereal bowl with a funny figure at the bottom of the bowl. I ate rapidly just so I could see the figure. That's the kind of initial feeling one should get—and the kind of feeling one should retain—about furnishings."

He goes on building our confidence, saying, "Really good design is something you don't get tired of. You appreciate it more and more as time goes by. I'm not talking about silly furniture. I'm talking about things you admire from some standpoint for a long time. Things you have a deep admiration for. Perhaps it's a beautiful piece of inlaid wood and the workmanship that goes along with it." Fine, fine—then we find that this connoisseur of non-silly furniture is busy selling a blood-red divan made of foam polyurethane and covered in stretch nylon in the shape of an enormous pair of LIPS. You sit on the pouty lower lip and hope to God the thing doesn't gobble you up. Of course, it would be great for a party—you could line up white vinyl throw pillows on it to give a smiling effect early in the evening, insert a large rubber cigar for an after-dinner mood, and finally jab in a mannequin's leg for a ghoulish touch designed to drive out hangers-on. That might be fun for *one party*; for every day, hardly. Unless you are a lip fetishist, you would not be likely to appreciate this divan more and more as time goes by. It's a fad.

Fads may have lots of pizzazz, zip, zest. They are often fun and spark conversation among guests. They also wear out their welcome in a hurry, and you are left with a roomful of stale jokes.

Considering the delivery lag in buying furniture, you'll be lucky if the faddy furniture you order is still in style when you get it. Even at that, though, you would be better off than the show-business star who is reported to have furnished her living room with inflatable furniture; after a party, she found her room furnished with punctured and flattened furniture.

Inflatables are notorious for squealing when sat upon, for blowing out under pressure and for just being too low to the floor. They also become too hot to sit on for any length of time. Portability just doesn't offset all these flaws.

Sofas that look like lips, inflatable furniture, beanbag chairs and waterbeds are all fads that definitely will not be on the shopping list of anyone who views furniture as a long-range investment.

Fads are novelties that are often stocked as impulse items in furniture stores. Beanbag chairs are piled up into a mountain of bright-colored vinyl right in the center of the store's traffic pattern. They catch the eye and the spur-of-the-moment buyer. Unhappily, fads are not always low-priced. Much of what is billed as "high-style" modern is merely faddish, but there is nothing mere about the price. Chrome phallic lamps, lamps that move and writhe about the floor, cocktail tables with live fish swimming in the base are all expensive fads.

A material may be a fad too. For example, chrome and glass enjoyed a great surge of popularity in the early seventies, and designers worked to use the combo in new—never mind appropriate—shapes. Some turned out Victorian rockers in chrome, others created the bamboo look in chrome. Fads.

THE EVER-POPULAR BORAX

"Borax" has been defined as anything so ugly it must sell. Makers of borax follow H. L. Mencken's warrant that "No one ever went broke underestimating the taste of the American people." There are those who define borax as "mass-produced," meaning produced for the masses. Very often the most popular movie, novel or play is one that the critics damned but the masses loved. So it is with borax. Although you will not find borax included in any list of furniture styles, it is a definite and consistent part of the home furnishings scene. No matter what style is in current favor, borax is always with us. There are manufacturers who proudly declare their lines to be borax, and some dealers call themselves Borax Kings—all in confidence to the trade, of course. Nobody advertises his stuff to the public as borax.

There is no one outstanding identifying trait of borax. Rather, it is the sum of its parts—shoddy materials, flamboyant colors, a callous disregard of craftsmanship and a total absence of aesthetic appeal. A sofa featuring slabs of foam rubber for cushions, orange Orlon fun fur as upholstery fabric and wood-look plastic finials for trim is borax. Lurex glitter upholstery is borax. It is almost invariably low-priced and is offered to dealers as "promotional."

Any furniture style can be translated into borax. The recent popularity of Mediterranean-style furniture offered borax makers an unprecedented chance to plummet to the depths of creativity. Bedroom sets became masterpieces of vulgarity as they grew bulkier and more heavily encrusted with molded-plastic "carving." Headboards featured inserts of Lurex or lamé glittering behind "gold" grillework. Chests bore a striking resemblance to upended coffins.

Borax is generally found in inner-city stores that cater to low-income shoppers, but it turns up in suburban stores as well and, if you've been looking, you know that Sears, Montgomery Ward and Penney's all carry their share too. It is often sold in room packages—"all five gorgeous pieces for our unbelievably low, low price."

No matter how low the price, how many pieces in the package or how bright the colors, borax is never a good buy. It is poorly made, the materials used are low quality, and it will not wear well. Even if you like the way it looks—and obviously many people do—don't buy it.

WHAT STYLE TO BUY?

If you should never buy borax, what should you buy? Of course, a decorator may be of great help in solving many furnishing problems (see Chapter 5), but you should have some idea of the particular style you prefer before consulting a decorator.

Millions of words have been written on how to choose furniture to express yourself—the real you. Broyhill Furniture gushes in its brochure *What Every Girl Should Know About Furniture Buying*, "You want a style that stands right up on its toes and sings out the fact that it's you!" *The Complete Family Interior Decorating Book* (Curtin Promotions, Inc., 1972) begins chapter one enthusiastically: "You're about to embark on a great adventure—decorating a room, an apartment, possibly a whole house . . . You, the homemaker, probably spend more time in your home than any other member of the family. It's your background and should reflect your personality." This publication then offers a five-question quiz (your favorite time of day, your favorite colors, your favorite fabrics, your kind of party, your favorite "on the town" clothes) to peg you to a furniture "look."

More imaginatively, other writers turn to astrology and use the signs of the zodiac to link furniture styles to individuals. (Scorpio: Do you yearn to travel to romantic, mysterious places; do you whip up paella and serve it by candlelight? You're a Mediterranean girl!)

All such quizzes and gimmicks are about as reliable as paper crutches. They are dreamed up by writers whose goal is next week's paycheck, not the mutual suitability of you and your furniture. They may be fun to read, but should not be taken seriously.

When selecting a style for your home, you must first take a long, hard look at your needs. Certainly, if you live alone, then you can indulge in your personal preferences. If, however, you share your home with one or more other people, their needs must also be considered. That is, you may see yourself as a Marie Antoinette type deserving of satin brocades and crystal; but you may be a Marie Antoinette with six kids who would demolish that crystal in an instant.

If you are furnishing an entire house, take the project on a room-by-room basis. Consider each room in terms of its use. Will you be entertaining in the living room or in the family room? Will you be using your living room for nightly TV and popcorn? Do you need that third bedroom, or could it be more useful as a den? Will you be having overnight guests often? Do the kids have an area for roughhousing? Do you enjoy giving large dinner parties?

Look ahead, too. Will the kids be entertaining at home in a few years? Will they be leaving home soon? Will you be having more kids?

How about your family's approach to daily life? Are you a casual, easygoing family with drop-in friends and spur-of-the moment gatherings? Or are you more the plan-ahead, a-place-for-everything-and-everything-in-its-place type?

Finally, upkeep and maintenance should be considered when choosing a furniture style. Is your family hard on furniture? If you are active outside the home, with little time for housework, you will want to focus on furnishings that require the minimum of upkeep.

Once you've established your priorities, you may turn to considering furniture styles. A quick trip to the library will provide you with dozens of books on furniture styles. The *Encyclopedia of Furniture* (Crown Publishers, Inc., 1965) by Joseph Aronson, is a particularly good reference book. Browse through a few books and get an idea of what appeals to you immediately and what styles you absolutely loathe. Then look at the styles you like in terms of your own home and needs.

THE BIG THREE

You will soon find, generally speaking, that most furniture being made today fits into one of three categories: traditional, provincial and modern.

Traditional

"Traditional" in the commercial market generally refers to designs inspired by seventeenth- and eighteenth-century English designers. These designs have been distilled by time, and the true classics have filtered down to us today. Furniture purists snobbishly hold that after the Empire period (early nineteenth century), furniture styles became "degraded."

Queen Anne, Georgian, Chippendale, Hepplewhite, Sheraton and Federal American are popular traditional styles. Since we are using only three broad categories in our discussion, French styles such as Louis XIV, Louis XV, Louis XVI and Directoire must also be included under "traditional."

You may be sure that, whether it is ornate or simple, a good reproduction of a traditional design will never go out of style. It has lasted this long, and it isn't going to drop out now.

As prices of authentic antiques soar, period reproductions are seen grabbing a hefty share of the high-end furniture business. Affluent customers look at such reproductions as long-term investments, to be enjoyed today and passed on to coming generations.

If you have a young, growing family, you should remember that most traditional furniture features exposed wood that will get scratched and dented under hard wear. Also, chairs such as the popular Queen Anne wing chair, perched on graceful, curving high legs, do not withstand the heavy rocking or tipping kids like.

Classic florals, velvets and stripes in satin, damask and chintz are authentic upholstery materials, and modern manufacturers are doing a good job of making these stain-resistant. Rooms furnished in traditional style are usually gracious, formal and conservative.

Traditional upholstered furniture has often been deliberately blurred by manufacturers into something called transitional or contemporary. Transitional cannot be pigeonholed as any specific style, but goes well with any style. Often transitional furniture is said to be reminiscent of a certain style. Like a mongrel dog, it may be attractive and pleasing in its own way, but it carries no breed's pedigree. Sofas particularly are homogenized in this fashion.

Generally speaking, the good-looking traditional furniture is found in the middle-to-upper price ranges. When it is found in low-priced lines—and that's not often—it looks offensively low-priced. All that exposed wood and carving require care and craftsmanship not available at low cost. Like the little girl with the curl, when traditional furniture is good, it is very, very good . . . and when it is bad, it is horrid.

Provincial

Provincial is the most popular group of furniture in the United States today. It is usually called the offspring or adaptation of the more formal traditional designs, but it has in reality come a long way beyond that.

The most popular provincial style is what is commonly called Early American; however, Early American is an often-misused term. There is very formal *traditional* Early American furniture from the eighteenth and early nineteenth centuries. Such pieces were first adaptations of English styles from the Queen Anne, Chippendale and Sheraton periods; in the Federal period Duncan Phyfe, who is generally called the first American furniture designer, led the shift away from the English influence.

However, when the average shopper refers to Early American, she means the much more rustic, Colonial styles of maple, oak or pine. Ladder-back chairs, Hitchcock chairs, dry sinks and open hutches are typical Colonial items. Upholstered Colonial furniture tends toward plaids, tweeds, prints featuring eagles and flags, box-pleated skirts and shirring. Priscilla curtains, geraniums, copper teapots and milk-glass pieces are common accessories.

"Country Casual" is a popular invention of the furniture industry to capitalize on the popularity of both the Colonial and Mediterranean styles, which together grab up 50 per cent of the style market. Country Casual is the pub-and-club look—massive, rugged lines, without Colonial's curls or Mediterranean's carving. Oak, brass and parquet characterize Country Casual.

Mediterranean became extremely popular in the early sixties and only began to ease off ten years later. Heavily ornate, the dramatic style owes a strong debt to Spanish and Mexican designs. As designer O. B. Solie said, "The reign of Spain stays mainly not so plain." Baroque carving—more and more baroque as the price gets lower—massive lines, turned spindles, metal filigree, wrought-iron table bases, and velvet upholstery are the keys to identifying Mediterranean. Candles galore, Moorish wall plaques, and chains tend to find their way into Mediterranean settings.

Both Italian and French Provincial also belong in the broad, general Provincial category. Of all the Provincial styles, these two are the most formal and delicate and are seldom used throughout the house.

French Provincial is derived from the French court furniture of the eighteenth century, but is greatly simplified. Curved lines, cabriole legs, and painted fruitwood finishes create its graceful look.

Italian Provincial was an imitation of the furniture of the nobility of Italy at a time when classic Roman lines were in fashion. Straight, simple lines, fluted and grooved posts, and much exposed wood on upholstered pieces are now typical of this style. Today's Italian Provincial is most often seen in antique white with pale blue or lemon-yellow—and even apricot or peach—trim.

Certainly, provincial (Country Casual and Colonial) furniture is the number-one choice for family rooms—or what some designers pretentiously call the "informal activities room." For some reason, this room, more than any other, has undergone a series of name changes. First it was the rec. room or den, then the family room, and now that term too has become passé. As the name has changed, so have our attitudes toward the room. At one time it was typically furnished with castoffs from the living room. However, sales of furniture specifically for use in the family room have grown to such staggering proportions that some retailers report it as their hottest category.

Buyers generally focus on comfort and ease of maintenance in family room furniture. The massive lines of Country Casual furniture cater to the overstuffed, easy comfort wanted; and, if the furniture is well built, it will stand up to heavy use. Sturdy vinyl and tough synthetic tweeds resist wear and staining, and look good in casual styles.

Delicate-looking French Provincial in painted finishes is a perennial choice for little girls' rooms. Both Italian and French Provincial are usually upholstered in brocades or velvets; while these may be made stain-resistant, they are poor choices for hard-use areas.

To keep the cost down on some ornate Mediterranean groups, makers turned to the use of plastic panels and parts. (Then, when the cost of plastic went up, these same manufacturers started shifting to less ornate styles.) Of course, manmade materials are being used more frequently at all price levels, but the buyer should certainly be wary of the low-priced group with much use of plastic ornamentation (see Chapter 6).

Provincial styles are found in all price ranges. The more rustic Country and Colonial styles, particularly, are often interpreted quite well at reasonable prices. It is possible to carry out the Colonial or Country theme throughout an entire room—drapes, lamps and accessories— economically. Mediterranean, French Provincial and Italian Provincial demand a bit more in terms of materials and workmanship, and therefore are a bit more costly to accessorize.

Modern

Somewhat surprisingly, modern is over 50 years old. What tradition there is in modern furniture springs from the German Bauhaus school of arts and crafts of about 1925. Following the principle of "Form follows function" and linking furniture to architecture, the practitioners of the Bauhaus theories introduced tubular metal furniture, hand-woven fabrics and modular storage pieces. Scandinavian furniture—"Danish modern"—began to be an influence in the thirties. The Scandinavians are most noted for making wood, in itself, look beautiful. Their simple cabinet styles focused new attention on the lovely wood grains of walnut, teak, rosewood, and birch in oiled finishes.

Although modern styles are constantly evolving, there are definite modern classics that remain as fresh and new-looking today as they did when first introduced. First, predating even the Bauhaus school, Michael Thonet introduced the bentwood rocker in 1860. Today this classic is on permanent display in the Museum of Modern Art. The Barcelona chair, designed by Mies van der Rohe in 1929, is *de rigueur* in the most chic modern airports, galleries and living rooms. The free-flowing styles of Eero Saarinen and the molded plywood and leather chair by Charles Eames are certainly stellar modern classics. All of these disprove the oft-repeated notion that modern furniture goes out of style almost before you get it home. Good, basic design is timeless.

Of course, not all modern is of Mies van der Rohe quality, just as not all traditional meets Chippendale standards. Fine modern features the finest leather and fabric upholstery. When wood grain is a key design feature, the wood used must be of the best quality. The spare designs offer no hiding place for shoddy workmanship. All of this spells "expensive" . . . and we know that you can get cheap modern.

Foam-rubber slabs on dowel-rod legs, flash-and-dash colors and patterns, industrial-looking lighting—all of these have combined to give modern a basically undeserved second-class reputation. In *How to Invest in Beautiful Things Without Being A Millionaire* (David McKay Co., Inc., 1971) Elaine Cannel contends that "It is one of the amazing features of modern that no matter what material it is made of, it usually ends up looking as though it were made of plastic."

Certainly, the modern category is home to the most far-out, nutty designs that on the furniture actuarial tables would have a life span of three seconds before boredom at best and disgust at worst set in. Because the lines of the furniture are so simple, retailers often turn modern showrooms into a riot of bright colors, mirrors, metallic wallpapers, and pop-op posters. Wet-look vinyls, Orlon fun furs, and chrome trim too often serve as substitutes for quality construction and materials. When shopping for modern, you must mentally strip away such distractions and focus on the frequently-dismaying basics.

Bouncing around on the periphery of modern is the nostalgic Art Deco style. A trendy flashback to the twenties and thirties, Art Deco was the modern of that period. Puffy, squooshy, plush, lush chairs and plastic, chrome and glass are all part of the Art Deco look that is really a sort of traditional fad.

ORIENTAL AND VICTORIAN

Oriental and Victorian styles somehow seem to defy categorizing. The Oriental influence is seen in many furniture lines, but few to none may be said to be truly Oriental, and many are mere chop suey. Lacquered cabinets with Eastern-looking hardware, low snack tables or stools with turned-in legs, fretwork trim on straight-line pieces are said to be "Oriental." The Eastern influence is also interpreted in bamboo effects and cane trim. In fact, the bamboo look has been seen in everything from chrome to actual bamboo—although the latter is a rare exception. Covering all bases, or as many as possible anyway, one manufacturer has produced a vinyl-covered, button-tufted, strapped lounge chair with bamboo-look legs and cane paneling—sort of an overstuffed armchair for Mao Tse-tung's family room.

Romantic as an 1890's valentine, Victorian is seldom treated seriously as a full-fledged furniture style, but from time to time it reappears for a brief burst of interest, only to subside until the next wave of nostalgia washes over the furniture industry. If you are truly an enthusiastic ante-bellum buff lodged in the Deep South, this may be your "Early American." Otherwise, an occasional piece is more than enough.

ECLECTIC

You love to travel, but are happy to stay at home; you adore gingham but have a passion for cut velvet; Chippendale turns you on, but a hot-pink molded-plastic table is irresistible. You've taken all the quizzes and charted your horoscope and still haven't found the REAL YOU furniture style. No need to worry. "If you're a split personality in many ways," according to one style analyst, eclectic is for you. (Plus a session with the psychiatrist, one might assume.)

Eclectic is not a style on its own, but is a blend of various styles. It would seem that if you are stuck with a selection of Early Thrift Shop, Traditional Hand-Me-Down and Brand-New Modern, eclectic is almost inevitable. Deliberately embarking on an eclectic decorating scheme is a risky task unless you are very skilled or have the guidance of a professional decorator. Manufacturers do not offer you the safety of a perfectly scaled and matched eclectic group. You alone must harmonize wood tones, fabrics, sizes and styles—a hefty undertaking.

Eclectic is a definite boon to the retailer, because he can now steer the customer to anything-with-everything. If you come in looking for an Early American chair to go with your Early American room setting and the retailer hasn't got anything in that style that pleases you, he can now promote "eclectic" and suggest you take the fashionable route to blending his Mediterranean chair with your other pieces.

If you are determined to individualize your home in this style, it is best to combine pieces that are consistent with a general, established feeling—formal or informal. Then make sure that all the pieces chosen are in scale. That is, don't put a fragile Oriental tambouret table in front of an undulating Victorian love seat. Finally, find some thread of continuity, such as color, and stick with it, thus unifying the diverse components.

COLOR

Color is fun. It can be exciting, stimulating or relaxing. More important to the retailer, it sells.

Color sells like nothing else. Every year about February the consumer magazines go into an orgy of color issues, and trade magazines follow suit in a somewhat more restrained manner. The February 1974 issue of National Home Furnishings Association's *Reports* magazine for retailers was devoted to the theme "Color Can Make the Sale." Color in ads, color in display, but most of all, color in furniture itself is a vital ingredient in making sales.

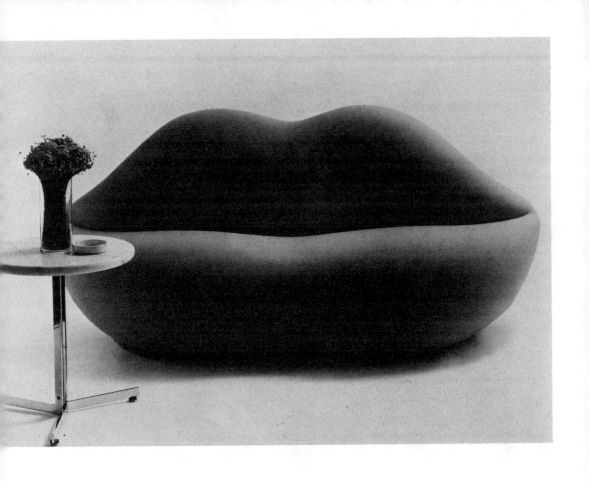

Smack! Smack! Love it for fun, but like any wary bachelor don't be lured by a pair of red lips into committing yourself to a long-range investment you may regret. *(Stendig)*

Massive Mediterranean combines Spanish, French and Italian influences to produce an American sales success. This piece is from the "Elegante" group, which in 1974 was reported as one of the top ten best-selling dining room groups in the United States. *(Keller Manufacturing)*

There's no mystery about this Hitchcock—it's an American classic. The arched, unusually turned top rail, the broad back panels and almost square seat are characteristic of the typical Colonial chair. The rush seat adds a nice Early American touch. *(Nichols & Stone)*

Colonial furniture is a perennial favorite that provides a cozy, casual look.
Enthusiasts of this style are fiercely loyal and tend to carry the Colonial theme
throughout the entire house.   *(DeSoto Furniture)*

"Country" is a cross between Colonial and Mediterranean. Oak, brass and carving keynote this look that probably will not have the staying power of Colonial.
(DeSoto Furniture)

The old standby daybed takes on modern functionalism here. It comes completely outfitted with quilted spread and matching bolsters—plus a concealed pop-up unit that provides sleeping for two.
(Kemp Furniture)

The ever-popular Thonet bentwood rocker disproves the notion that modern furniture goes out of style overnight. *(Thonet, Gebrüder. Rocking Chair. 1860. Bent beechwood; cane. 37½" high. Collection, The Museum of Modern Art, New York. Gift of Café Nicholson.)*

The renowned Barcelona chair designed by Mies van der Rohe in 1929. Further proof of the enduring qualities of good design. *(Knoll International)*

More than seven feet wide and almost eight feet high, this secretary-breakfront exemplifies fine-quality casegoods. No matter what price range you ultimately choose, first check out the craftsmanship, wood, finish, hardware and detailing of top-quality pieces. These standards should guide you in your final choice. *(Kittinger)*

Colorful displays can turn us on to a style we had not previously found interesting. As mentioned earlier: you will often find simple, straight-lined modern furniture featured in the brightest, most unusual prints and colors, and surrounded by equally colorful accessories and backgrounds. In the color-wise store display the sleek chrome chair looks utterly "modern-as-tomorrow." In your more conservatively-colored living room, it looks like something out of a dentist's office.

A guiding rule of most store designers is that the background sells the furniture. Furniture-store designer David Parmalee maintains that while high-quality wood furnishings should be surrounded by low-key colors to let the beauty of the wood hold the center of attention, lower-priced, less beautiful furnishings should be dressed up with strong, bright hues in a splashy background.

Color diverts the shopper from the sleaziness of upholstery fabric or from shoddy construction. Borax furniture is often offered in the most garish colors and fabrics. The manufacturers of home furnishings— particularly borax—have long known that people will sacrifice quality for a desired color. Not a wise move on the shopper's part, but sensational for the dealer.

Not only is color used to sell styles or qualities of furniture, but it is a salable item in itself. A survey conducted among 6,000 consumers by Leisure Time Research, Incorporated, and presented at a furniture conference in 1973 offered this conclusion: "Choice of colors is the single most important [area] of decorating ideas women seek . . . as mentioned by 59 per cent of all respondents." The Los Angeles *Times* queried 227 Los Angeles-area households on wall-to-wall carpeting. The results, released in February 1974, indicated that color is by far the most im-portant factor in the selection of carpet.

Tracking this powerful color influence is itself big business. The Color Association of the United States is ever busy tabulating and predicting our color preferences. This association's membership is composed of companies in a variety of retail and manufacturing businesses who meet annually with experts to determine the up-and-coming color trends.

More visible to the consumer is the long-running *House & Garden* annual color promotion. Since 1947 this magazine has been assuring manufacturers and consumers of the current color trends. In an ad to the trade headlined "Everything under the sun sells better in color," the magazine boasted, ". . . *House & Garden* delivers five million color-responsive readers. With high incomes, and even higher expectations and buying power. Receptive to ideas and products that represent color change. Identifiable as 'heavy user' consumers for color in the broadest range of home products. . . . [T]he March issue takes off where the September issue left off. Regenerating customer interest and buying action at the point of sale where more and more commodities are being promoted in *House & Garden* Colors. This spring the magazine's Sunshine Yellows promotion will brighten sales for department stores, home specialty stores and home improvement centers across the nation." And that's the point. Colors are not just noted and predicted; they are promoted and merchandised. *House & Garden* has over 600 major resources tied into its promotions, bombarding shoppers with Goldenrod, Space Blue, Beach Plum or whatever the color-of-the-year happens to be.

While your emotional and social values are kept in mind when colors are chosen by these pros, technology can also have a strong influence. The price of synthetic yarns varies according to color gradations, and white is cheapest. Therefore, white is often promoted as a big favorite. White turned up when Midge Wilson, executive director of the Color Association, explained industry's plan to cope with the energy crisis as it affected them in 1974. "For at least two years, white is going to be stressed in home furnishings and fashions. It won't be a hospital white, but softer, cream-colored hues such as Nacre Cream and Ivory Ice. By emphasizing white or cream, the dye industry won't have to rely so much upon coal chemicals, the textile factories won't have to worry about obtaining scarce, brightly-colored dyes, and the buying public will be exposed to a new fashion idea—whites again."

And, lo and behold, it all came to pass. White was featured throughout the media. DuPont headlined: "White, the newest color in fashion. Everywhere you look, white's in sight . . . in apparel . . . in the home . . . and it's right." Chirping over nostalgia, elegance, simplicity and taste, the ad writer heralded, "White is the newest color signal of the seventies. And it 'belongs' in the world around us." Indeed, in the dye-scarce world around us, at any rate.

Of course, Vance Packard made us all aware years ago that marketing experts have been using color in packaging to sell merchandise in supermarkets. We must be aware that we are being hustled with color by the home furnishings industry too.

Retailers love to see you invest in "dramatic" red sofas and "striking" print carpets. Chances are you will be back much sooner than your budget dictates to replace what has become a jangling, boring or overwhelming color choice. As you will see again in Chapter 8, too-bright colors and prints are prime movers in the planned-obsolescence concept. Color is a powerful force that you should definitely keep in mind when making the big-ticket decisions of furniture buying.

Happily, several factors—consumerism, women's lib, better education—have combined in recent years to make shoppers more resistant to buying items in the latest colors merely because they are the *latest* colors. In fact, the Color Association's 1971 report stated that the American woman "has rearranged her priorities. Function has become more important than fashion. She does not crave new fashions in rapid succession but rather variations on the theme which she can assimilate gradually and easily."

Buy what you like best, not what is being promoted this season. Parrot green and azalea pink may enchant *House & Garden* this spring, but you are stuck with them next season too. Don't buy a color unless it is your personal color for this year and years to come. To coin a copywriter's phrase, follow your personal rainbow.

How do you know what color or colors suit you best? There are seemingly legions of professionals whose careers are built on explaining, defining and analyzing color preferences. Psychologists have been linking color preferences to sex, financial and/or social status, age group, political situations and national crises for generations. Their dictates are familiar. "The higher the income, the greater the tendency to prefer subdued colors." "In times of economic recession people want bright, cheerful colors." "People are saving energy by turning off lights, so they need lighter colors." "Young people want daring, exciting colors." In *What Your House Tells About You* (Trident Press, Inc., 1973), interior designer Virginia Frankel pursues the classic theme: "People who like bright, hot or acid colors—oranges, reds, strong purples and greens—are often bold, adventurous, with-it, and generally happy. Blues and greens in the middle range can bespeak coolness, possibly conservativeness and caution. The use of beiges, grays and muddy pastels might connote a person unsure of himself, and a predominance of dark colors may be the sign of a night person, or one who is moody and depressed."

Somewhat more scientifically, a Swiss psychologist, Dr. Max Luscher, has compiled *The Luscher Color Test* (Random House, 1969) to detect

what your color preferences reveal about your personality. Color consultants are setting up shop in major cities; for a fee they will advise you as
to which colors will make you happier, sexier, calmer—whatever you
wish.

Critics of all of these color professionals point out that the whole
"science" has about as much validity as astrology. Take it for its worth. It
can be fun—we all like to analyze ourselves. But then sit down and use
some common sense. You know what your favorite colors are. *House
Beautiful* acknowledges that "Individual color preferences rarely
change." You get a good feeling from certain colors and react negatively
to others. Perhaps to the rest of the world yellow is warm, illuminating
and cheerful, but it reminds *you* of a terrible day when you were four and
the neighborhood bully wearing a yellow shirt wrecked your bike. So, no
matter what the color predictors cheer as the "warm, wonderful, witty"
color of the year, if you don't react positively, avoid it.

Remember the others in your family too. Check out their color
preferences. All too often husbands cop out by claiming, "Whatever you
decide is O.K. with me," and then, when everything is bought, delivered
and arranged, they agonize, "But I never thought you would buy a
hot-pink sofa. I hate pink."

When choosing a color scheme, you also should consider the use of the
room being decorated. Pale beiges and whites may be great for your
company-only living room, but a poor choice for the family room. Even
the soil-resistant finishes can't stand up to a daily onslaught of popsicles.

Colors can visually extend the size of a room, diminish the height of a
too-tall room, warm a bleak northern exposure or ease the glare of a
too-sunny one. Decorating books are filled with such tips.

When using these books, however, don't get carried off on the tide of
the decorator's enthusiasm. Cut out all those adjectives and flowery
phrases—"Red says welcome as appealingly as a fire on the hearth,"
"cool, serene, blue," "rich and burnished gold—bold but not brassy,"
"go-everywhere gray"—and substitute your own.

Neutrals, of course, are excellent choices for major purchases that you
do not intend to replace for several years. You can mix and match many
other colors with them, thus changing the appearance of the room
without a big investment. For example, a beige carpet and sofa can be
sparked with orange and white occasional chairs, orange pillows and
accessories for one look, and can work equally well with green, turquoise,
gold, or brown for a fresh, new look. Get as much mileage as possible
from your color choice.

MAKE A TEST RUN

After you have selected those styles and colors you think you want to use in furnishing your home, check them out in actual use—before you buy. Visit models of new homes and apartments and model-room settings in stores. When you visit friends' homes, pay attention to their choices of colors and styles. Note your emotional response to rooms done in certain colors: how do you "feel" surrounded by, say, Italian Provincial? What seemed ideal on paper may, in practice, be quite wrong for you. A small person may feel dwarfed by immense Jacobean or Mediterranean pieces; a large person may feel twice as large surrounded by dainty French period pieces. An all-white living room may appear cool and sophisticated in magazines, but you may feel as though you're in an igloo when you actually visit such a room.

FOUR

Where To Shop

You know what you can spend and what you want to spent it on. Now, where do you go to spend it? In the summer of 1973 Sylvia Porter, the well-known financial columnist, wrote, "Furniture buying is the number-one agony in the United States today." That's a rather drastic statement in view of the problems of poverty, crime, old age, housing and pollution, but it does serve to emphasize the very real fact that buying home furnishings can be a frustrating, time-consuming project.

FULL-SERVICE TO NO-SERVICE

Much of that frustration and wasted time can be eliminated by shopping at dealers who answer your particular needs. There are, of course, several kinds of stores that sell home furnishings, and within the different categories stores vary in quality and service. Certain generalizations, however, can be made.

First, you may want to shop at the *full-service store*. The full-service store used to be known simply as a furniture store. Then the warehouse-showroom came along, picked up the furniture store by the scruff of its profit margin and gave it a good shaking. The new name—full-service store—is one result of that shaking, and it's not a bad one. The store does offer more service than any other kind of furniture dealer. Custom orders, decorator counseling, in-home selling, well-trained sales personnel and satisfaction-guaranteed merchandise are some of the services customarily offered by many of these stores. Others may offer free decorating classes or seminars on furniture care.

This is the store that will permit you to order your sofa in just the right length to fit your room, to choose a loose pillow-back or channel-back, to pick cover fabric from a rack of hundreds of swatches or to select the shade of the wood finish on the base.

Often family operations, full-service furniture stores make up the largest segment of the retail furniture industry, and most shoppers will visit at least one when considering a furniture purchase—especially shoppers who have not made up their minds as to what they want. Research has shown that undecided shoppers turn to furniture stores because they want to examine a wide selection of different styles, materials and colors, and believe the full-service store can provide such a selection.

What are the problems of buying from a full-service store? For one thing, such stores face stiff price competition from those who can purchase in large lots, thus obtaining a lower per-unit price. The little guy is often outpriced in dollar-for-dollar comparisons. To meet this competition many dealers are now considering hooking up with buying syndicates. By doing so the dealer can pool his buying needs with those of others and through bulk buying get a price break from the manufacturer. He will also get advice from the syndicate on advertising, selling and management.

The biggest complaint, though, is delivery—and it's not the retailer's fault. After selling a shopper a $1,500 dream dining room set, the dealer then has to explain that she will have to wait three months—or longer—for that dream to become a reality. In April 1973 the National Association of Furniture Manufacturers reported the average delivery time for casegoods (dressers, tables, breakfronts, etc.) was 15.4 weeks—the longest wait recorded in the five years the NAFM had kept records. In 1973 people were waiting about six weeks longer for casegoods than they ever had before. The upholstery situation was better—but not much. The upholstery delivery time averaged 8.8 weeks.

There are many excuses offered by the industry for this situation. Manufacturers point to shortages of materials and skilled labor, but a Better Business Bureau spokesman pointed out that manufacturers often deliberately delay production of furniture items until sufficient orders have been accumulated, because "It's more economical for them this way." Retailers add that manufacturers have not planned ahead and are working from outgrown and outmoded factories. Whatever the excuse or fault, the little retailer and the consumer get caught in the Big Wait.

Obviously, if a retailer is going to offer the shopper the option of a custom-made purchase, he can't warehouse dozens of sofas in the hope that she'll choose one of them and thus have instant delivery. Custom orders are individually placed with the manufacturer at the time of purchase. Also, warehousing requires a great deal of space and is too costly for most retailers to attempt on an adequate scale.

The *specialty shop* is generally a small or independent operation which shares many of the qualities of the full-service store. The big difference is that the specialty store features only one segment of the home furnishings field, such as carpets, lamps or tables. Such stores certainly are most likely to feature the widest range of stock within their specialized fields. However, research has shown that it generally takes a really single-minded, sophisticated and experienced shopper to be contented with shopping in a specialty store. The shopper in a lamp store, for example, cannot place the lamp she is considering next to a chair or on a table to get an idea of how it might fit into her own home. She must examine the lamp among dozens of other lamps of all sizes, shapes and colors, with little or no clue to its suitability for her home.

For this reason many specialty operators are adding little room vignettes to their displays. This is some help, but does not entirely solve the problem. Only a limited number of vignettes can be presented. In a lamp store that might mean featuring eight or nine lamps in small settings . . . and leaving a couple of hundred on the shelf.

Depending on his warehouse facilities and the amount of money he is willing and able to invest in back-up stock, the specialty store operator's delivery situation is about on a par with that of the full-service store.

The *department store* offers a third alternative for the furniture shopper. A big plus factor for the department store is its familiarity to consumers from their past purchases of a wide range of merchandise. The store's ways, layout and policies are familiar, and this helps to make an uncertain shopper feel more "at home" as she makes her decisions. If the department store enjoys a reputation for quality and you have been satisfied with your purchases and the treatment you have received from the store, you are likely to return there for home furnishings.

Davison's, a chain of department stores in the South, recently went in for home furnishings in a big way and at that time spelled out what it saw as the big advantages of department stores as home furnishings centers. It first cited customer acceptance and then went on to say that department stores can feature well-known and exclusive brands which standard furniture stores do not have the buying power to obtain. Davison's also claimed that "discriminating customers" recognize that the "discount umbrella" under which the price-specialists operate is not always real.

For many years only "quality" department stores offered custom and decorator services in their home furnishings departments, but in the past few years the giants—Sears, Montgomery Ward and Penney's—have added these services too.

Department stores, like full-service and specialty stores, may offer careful delivery and a setup service without extra charge (you already paid for it in the purchase price)—a point worth remembering unless you like to move furniture. Many such stores specially train their delivery men not only to set up and inspect the furniture being delivered, but also to place it as the customer wishes. This means that if they are delivering a sofa, for example, and the buyer wants every piece of furniture in her living room moved to accommodate it, the delivery men will move it and keep moving it until she is happy.

On the "con" side of department store shopping, many customers are likely to find the large store impersonal and rather overwhelming. Many shoppers complain that salespeople "float" from department to department and, as a result, are not knowledgeable about the merchandise. Also, unless the store is a real whopper, its selection of home furnishings is apt to be rather limited. Like the full-service store, the department store is generally subject to the perils of delivery from manufacturers.

The *warehouse-showroom* offers an alternative to the delivery problem. There, what you buy today *you* take home today. Such availability of merchandise has boosted the warehouse-showroom into a near $1-billion-a-year business.

It all began in Pottsdown, Pennsylvania, where the Levitz family ran furniture stores. Leon Levitz opened a store in Tucson, Arizona, and in 1953 was in financial difficulty with it. Brother Ralph Levitz packed his bags, went to Tucson and, with his brother, staged a successful warehouse sale. On his return to Pottsdown, Ralph ran more and more warehouse sales until the sales became a merchandising concept that shook the home furnishings industry.

Levitz has now been joined in the warehouse-showroom business by many other companies, all operating on the same basic principles. The stores all do business out of football-field-size warehouses. The shopper enters through the warehouse, passing tier upon tier of furniture. The showrooms feature literally hundreds of fully-accessorized room settings under bright overhead lights. Some dealers group the settings by function—that is, all living rooms, dining rooms, bedrooms together. Others group by style—modern, Mediterranean, Colonial.

The price tag is usually a three- or four-part deal, itemizing the options: "deluxe" or "custom" price (includes delivery, unpacking, and setup); or the warehouse-showroom price, plus the additional cost of delivery and another cost for setup. The shopper chooses the piece she wants, places the order, and, by the time she has paid for it and driven her car to the loading dock, the purchased piece is waiting for her.

It is this immediate availability that is the greatest motivation in drawing customers to the warehouse-showrooms. According to Wickes Corporation, a giant firm with warehouse-showrooms in the Midwest, there are many people who are willing to say, "I'll take that and I'll take it today," even if their choices are not exactly what they first had in mind.

In addition to instant availability, price is a big draw at the warehouse-showrooms. The warehouse operations are promoted as selling for less, and they often—but not always—do. There are several reasons for this. The warehouse eliminates almost all of the costly services offered by the traditional retailer. But without paying extra for it, the customer usually cannot get predelivery preparation, storage for later delivery, scheduled-in-advance delivery, setup in the home, decorating service or easy credit. Since the traditional retailer has begun to recognize anew his own good qualities in these areas and has started to promote them with vigor, the warehouse-showroom has countered by including many services in the base price. Of course, that in turn raises the base price and narrows the gap between the traditional retailer and the warehouse-showroom.

The warehouse-showroom is able to achieve lower prices through volume. It buys 500 or 600 items from a single manufacturer, not five or six items as the small retailer must. This bulk buying lowers the unit cost, and carload rates reduce freight charges.

What are some of the drawbacks a shopper may encounter at the typical warehouse-showroom? She may not like the assembly-line, crowded atmosphere or the lack of services available. For all the hullabaloo about selection, she won't find anything but do-it-yourself carpet there. An exception to this situation occurs when the warehouse-showroom operator leases space within his store to a carpet dealer. If you consider buying from such a dealer, don't assume that the warehouse-showroom's reputation, standards or rules apply to the carpet seller. That can be a whole new deal altogether. Check the carpet dealer's return, refund and exchange policies before you buy.

In some warehouse-showrooms you won't find full dining room or bedroom sets displayed. Instead of "wasting" valuable showroom floor space on the entire set, the warehouse-showroom features one or two pieces and a color photograph of the rest. You are not at all likely to find appliances or TV's at a warehouse-showroom. Why not? Warehouse-showroom operators don't want the hassle of service, installation or maintenance. If you should come across a warehouse-showroom selling carpets, appliances or TV sets, those departments are probably operated by a franchised dealer. That is, the warehouse operator subcontracts space to a carpet dealer. If you decide to buy, you had better know who you are buying from and what his ground rules are on returns, refunds, exchanges and credit.

Further, credit is not easily obtained at many of these huge operations. Wickes has found that 70 per cent of its customers pay cash (but they usually buy only one item), and the remaining 30 per cent are offered one revolving-credit plan.

What about returns and refunds? If you buy a sofa at a warehouse-showroom, lash it to the top of your car and careen on home with it, only to find that it clashes terribly with your carpet, what can you do? Although warehouse-showrooms differ in detail, it is a general rule that you will have to get that sofa back to the warehouse within 24 hours for a refund. (Some dealers will never refund, only exchange.) What if you haul a breakfront home and find the side badly nicked? Get it back to the dealer immediately and hope he will believe the manufacturer did it. Maybe he will and maybe he won't.

Other retailers bitterly contend that much of the warehouse-showrooms' stocks are custom-ordered and are not as high in quality as the manufacturers' regular lines. It is true that by virtue of their size these operations can order special items not in the manufacturers' regular lines. This, of course, makes the consumer's comparison shopping impossible.

The warehouse-showroom operator aims his stock at the mass market. He is not interested in top-of-the-line, high-style or avant-garde furniture because, although there is a definite market for such goods, this market is not large enough to make it profitable for him. So, if you don't want the styles offered the "common market," steer clear.

Finally, if after careful planning on the cost, style, color and size of your furniture purchase, you switch just so you can have your purchase immediately, you have done yourself a disservice. It may mean that getting it quicker will only result in having longer to regret it.

Good or bad, the warehouse-showroom is here and is going to be part of the home furnishings scene for a long time to come. In fact, industry leaders have predicted that there will be a major shakeup of furniture stores by 1980—with the warehouse-showroom and national chains making survival difficult for the full-service store. C. J. Klinger, vice president of Wickes, sees the situation as being parallel to that of the food store: "Where once every block had its own ma-and-pa grocery, most are gone, and now there are supermarkets and gourmet and specialty shops. The same thing is happening in furniture retailing. The supermarkets are the warehouses; the gourmet shops are the more expensive, custom-order stores; and the specialty shops are those that offer decorating services and high-style designs. The middle-price, general home furnishings retailer is on the way out."

The *catalog-showroom* takes the self-service, do-it-yourself delivery concept a step further than the warehouse-showroom. Like shoppers at the warehouse-showroom, the catalog-showroom customer has the option of taking the merchandise with her or having it delivered at an extra cost. She may also pay an extra charge for setup service. The big difference between the two operations is that the catalog-showroom buyer gets a catalog to browse through at home and can then go to the showroom to get an "in the upholstery" look at her selection before buying. She will get little aid or interference—depending upon her point of view—from sales personnel.

While this catalog-showroom concept is new for home furnishings, it has been around for quite a while for jewelry, appliances and toys. In fact, it seems to be further proof of the axiom "The more things change, the more they stay the same." After all, Sears and Montgomery Ward got started as strictly catalog operations and then added retail outlets. Today retailers are adding catalogs to their stores.

Furniture Catalog Centers, New York, New York, is seen as the pioneer of this latest catalog technique. The firm uses its initials—FCC— throughout the catalog. Although perfectly legal, this does seem a rather sneaky way of suggesting responsibility—even a quasi-official status—by associating the firm with the Federal Communications Commission. This firm offers a discount for waiting for any merchandise that is out of stock, and, if the waiting period exceeds 30 days, the catalog states that an additional discount will be given.

The catalog-showroom idea is being taken up by companies of all kinds. Even an oil company, Cities Service Oil Company, is in the game and has opened a combination gas station-catalog-showroom in Rockville Centre, New York. This company obviously doesn't push service, image or glamour, but does stress price. It states that customers can buy at 5 per cent above CitGo's purchase price—and it offers a refund of the difference and a $1 bonus if prices are lower elsewhere. The catch here is a $10 membership fee. As Earl Lifshey says in his "If You Ask Me" column in *Home Furnishings Daily,* "Why anyone would—or should be expected to—pay for the privilege of spending his own money for merchandise in a closed-door, so-called discount store when he can always do as well or better elsewhere has long been one of life's minor mysteries. But then as Barnum put it, 'There's one born every minute.' "

The *discount club* has various forms. Some clubs charge membership fees; others are open only to members of unions, to certain corporations or to employees of the government. These operations claim they can save the shopper money on all purchases. Usually a smart shopper can, by comparison shopping, get the same deal—and even better—independently. Critics also claim that the clubs offer few brand-new items and that refunds range from difficult to impossible to obtain.

It is also true that the "closed door" to nonmembers is not very firmly closed. Membership cards are freely traded and in some cases given out by the store to anyone with the yen to buy. Although there have been numerous closed-door discount clubs, few endure for many years.

Finally, the *home center*, a new entrant into the home furnishings field, presently concentrates on floor coverings, with few if any items of furniture. Plywood Minnesota, Forest City and Wickes Lumber Centers are some of the big-chain home centers that mix do-it-yourself and prepackaged floor coverings with wall paneling, lumber, plumbing and electrical supplies. Whatever floor coverings the traditional floor-coverings specialty store doesn't carry, the home center almost certainly does. It offers a limited selection of carpet tiles and foam-backed carpet in the low-to-middle price range for the do-it-yourselfer who is not concerned with in-store service, delivery or installation.

Which of the various kinds of furniture outlets you choose to shop at will depend upon a variety of factors, including your own personality and the item you plan to buy. Certainly, if you are planning to establish a new living room look and want an overall plan established, detailing color, style and layout, you should turn to the full-service store for interior design service, custom-ordered furniture and trained delivery and setup. If you are uncertain and may wish to return your purchase, stay with this type of store or the department or specialty store. Go to these three for the installation of carpet too.

On the other hand, if you want to buy new bunk beds for the kids, want to shop without a lot of salesperson razzmatazz and want your purchase NOW, you will probably be happy at the warehouse-showroom. Of course, you can buy other, more expensive furniture there too—but don't sacrifice services you may need later for immediate possession or a *few* dollars' saving. For many dollars, O.K.

If you want credit, you can obtain it at most home furnishings outlets, but most credit shoppers turn to the full-service store or the specialty store for more flexible terms or better payment plans. Phone around to check on credit policies before you go out to buy, if this is the way you are going to pay.

You might assume that the price-conscious shopper would be most likely to prowl the discounters, warehouses and catalog-showrooms, but a recent study by the S & H Company found that price-conscious shoppers-—who make up 25 per cent of the furniture-buying public—are most likely to visit a Sears, Montgomery Ward or Penney's store.

WHO CAN YOU TRUST?

No matter what type of store you choose to buy from, you should make every effort to establish the firm's reliability. The less you know about home furnishings and the larger your purchase, the more important it is that you choose a store you can trust.

A reputable firm will stand behind the merchandise it sells. If you buy a recliner that refuses to recline, the reputable firm will replace it, at no cost to you. The dealer will not direct you to the manufacturer for replacement. He will guarantee and service the recliner for you and seek reparation from the manufacturer for himself.

A reputable dealer will put his guarantees or warranties in writing, and, if there are any specific limitations—such as those on sale merchandise—he will make sure you are aware of them at the time of purchase.

Most home furnishings dealers work hard to establish a clientele that will return time and again over the years. To do this they avoid high pressure and devious sales techniques, and instead stress service and quality. They are, like other businesses, out to make a buck, of course, but not by cheating you.

It is, however, an undeniable fact that they aren't *all* good guys. Gyp artists selling low-grade furniture at high prices and higher interest rates open for business every day in every kind of area. Hucksters can work the affluent suburb as well as the inner city.

To find a reputable dealer you can ask family, friends and neighbors where they have shopped and received good treatment; you can check with the local Better Business Bureau or a national trade association. The National Home Furnishings Association is an organization of furniture retailers; while not all reputable firms are members, those who are, are generally interested in improving the standards of the industry and are consumer-aware. The National Retail Merchants Association is a similar association of department stores.

THE MESSAGE IN THE MEDIA

You can also check home furnishings stores' advertisements for indications of reliability, as well as for price bracket, style or quality. Generally speaking, these stores concentrate their advertising budgets in newspapers, with direct mail the second favorite medium for reaching the public. This means you have printed ads to study and compare at your leisure. You can save yourself legwork and learn a great deal—more, in many cases, than the advertisers intend—by reading ads.

First, look at the numbers. Is the store within your price range? Discounters and warehouses make sure the price is up there in big bold numbers because, more than anything else, price is what they are selling. However, price is meaningless unless you know what it includes. For example: "Handsome 14-piece living room grouping—$395." (Of course, you're not mouse-trapped into thinking that's $300 instead of $400.) The ad shows a "luxurious" completely-furnished living room. Start counting and compare the text with the illustration. What are the 14 pieces included in the $395 price? Sofa, matching chair, three tables, two lamps, two pictures, two pillows, a 9 X 12 rug and . . . what? Surely the pair of occasional chairs in the illustration make the total 14. No. NO? The little round bolsters nestled next to the sofa arms make the total 14. That pair of occasional chairs is "available at a special price," it says in teeny-weeny type at the bottom of the ad. People in the trade lump such ads in with the joke ad for "55-piece living room," which consists of a sofa, two chairs and a deck of cards.

This practice of including an item of furniture in an illustration but not in the advertised price is quite common—especially in the ads for bedroom groups. A full-page ad promotes in inch-high letters: "HERE IT IS! SUPER SPECIAL New Romantic Mediterranean Master Bedroom. 5 Beautiful Pieces for $299." The illustration shows a dresser, mirror, chest, bed and nightstand—five beautiful pieces, but not the five available for $299. The chest is another "special price" deal, and the fifth included piece is the "sturdy steel frame on casters." It's surprising that the retailer doesn't tally up the four casters and make it a nine-piece group. Then there's the retailer who doesn't even itemize; he just waits until the shopper gets into the store to break the news that what the shopper sees in the ad is *not* what she gets for the price.

"Oh, well," retailers scoff. "This is nothing compared to the stuff they used to get away with in ads." Right—but the fact that it exists at all in this era of militant consumerism seems to indicate that the industry holds firm to an abiding faith in the stupidity of the shopper. As Ralph Nader has charged, too often furniture advertising is "written deliberately not to give information and to deceive."

MARKDOWNS, MONEY-SAVERS AND RIP-OFFS

The Federal Trade Commission and state bureaus of consumer protection have been busy watchdogging furniture advertising, and through these efforts many deceptive practices have been dropped or at least curtailed. Falsely advertised price "reductions," or "comparisons" and bogus sales are consumer traps that are under fire but have not yet been eliminated.

Under FTC guidelines, a legitimate price reduction must be, in fact, lower than the amount previously charged. That may seem obvious, but some dealers have claimed reductions from prices they never sold at— the "suggested retail price" is a variation on this gimmick. Others don't reduce prices at all, but only claim to do so. The item has always sold for $159, but suddenly a sale is on and it is available for the "special price" of $159. Also, sale prices must be of limited duration. If an item sells for $59.95 for a long period of time, then $59.95 becomes the regular—not sale—price of that item.

A store may advertise that its "special" price is lower than the "manufacturer's list price" or "suggested retail price." This is valid only if a substantial number of retailers in the area actually sell the item for that suggested price. All too often the manufacturer has posted a price that no one ever sells at—or is expected to sell at. This violates the FTC rules.

Warehouse-showrooms have been notorious for advertising comparatives: "regular price $199.95—now $149.95"; "sold elsewhere at $295.95—Blank's special price, $239.95." Frequently these claims cannot be substantiated and are, in fact, fictitious. Levitz has been charged with being an offender in this area, but government pressures have elicited a pledge to avoid such ad practices in the future.

Until the FTC and consumer protection agencies are able to eliminate such stunts permanently, it is up to the shopper to protect herself. Too many consumers are fleeced because they want to believe the deceptive ad. Don't be gullible. Stop believing that you might be getting something for nothing.

Read an ad, don't just skim it. Count the illustrated pieces and compare them with the text. Unfortunately, the only way to know if an item is really being offered at a reduced price is to know the market and prevailing prices. It's not easy. If you find a deceptive ad, you are forewarned that the store will probably follow through with deceptive practices on the sales floor. Stay away.

Hand-in-wallet with price, ads can clue you to the quality of the merchandise carried by a specific store. While price is certainly not the sole or most reliable index to quality (see Chapter 2), it is an indicator. The quality or "class" home furnishings store generally favors an airy ad with low-key copy. Price is discussed discreetly, if at all, and quality, performance and style are stressed. Designer services are often offered, and the brand names mentioned are tops.

Indications of quality may also be tied in with the advertised philosophy of the store. Some dealers make a point of running institutional ads citing their beliefs regarding customer satisfaction, decorating and lifestyles. An ad by The Designer's Shop in suburban Chicago typifies this approach: "We don't believe in dining room sets. Any more than we believe in living room sets. We think DINING is just as personal as sitting or sleeping, and so we buy the best tables, the best-designed chairs, the best storage and serving pieces (from whoever happens to make them). Then we have people with taste and imagination to help you put together the things you like. Exciting new things like olive ash burl and African Mozambique wood and sparkling chrome, and thick slabs of glass and gleaming lacquered colors. And exciting old things like marble and leather and velvet and walnut and rosewood. After all, why shouldn't your dining room be exciting?"

After reading this ad, you can expect the store to offer fairly stiff prices, an individualized approach, good quality, decorator service and a rather relentlessly with-it attitude. Of course, if you are an avowed believer in dining room sets and want it all manufacturer-coordinated, this is not the store for you.

This particular store bills itself as "one of the best modern stores in the country." Others may claim, "largest selection of Early American in the area." There is no point in wasting your time searching among calico-covered sofas and milk-pail lamps for a lemon-yellow plastic Parsons table. If you know what style furniture you are interested in, you will find the largest selection of that style at a store that specializes in it. Ads can lead you there.

A dealer who advertises his philosophy will probably stress his reliability and concern for your satisfaction too. John M. Smyth, an independent chain, builds much of its sales lure on this oft-repeated guarantee: "A LONG-ESTABLISHED SMYTH POLICY . . . is the [customer's] privilege of returning any piece of furniture she feels just does not look right when it has been delivered to her home. It is never necessary that a piece of furniture be damaged or defective for it to be returned to John M. Smyth Company. Complete satisfaction is thus guaranteed every Smyth customer in a meaningful way."

Ads can also help you when you are ready to buy specific items of furniture, and that is discussed in Chapter 6.

FIVE

Interior Designers

You're fascinated by Spanish styles, but you don't want your bedroom to look like the local branch office of the Inquisition. How do you avoid it?

You carefully outfitted your studio apartment in beige and white, but instead of looking palely elegant, it looks like petrified oatmeal. What can you do?

You chose excellent reproductions of authentic antiques, and now your living room looks like a museum. How do you make it look like a home?

Or perhaps you have ideas, but no confidence—or confidence, but no ideas. What can you do?

The answer to any and all of the above is, Get an interior designer's advice. (Interior designers used to be known as "decorators," but that term was deemed too frivolous a few years back.) At best a designer can save you time and money while making your dream home a reality. His knowledge of available current styles can send him directly to the source needed. You eliminate hours of shopping at stores that simply don't carry the styles or quality you want. The designer may also have color charts and fabric swatches available in his office, thus easing the decision-making process. He has access to those lines of home furnishings sold "to the trade only."

The designer, through accurate measurements and floor plans, can avoid costly errors. He may charge you only a small percentage over his

51

cost for an item, bringing the total to less than you would have paid on your own at retail. He can choose furnishings that are well made and durable, thus giving more wear for your dollar. He also can select pieces that you are not likely to tire of quickly—again providing longer life for your furnishings dollar.

At worst, an interior designer can bankrupt you without providing quality interior design. A poor designer can make the same mistakes you could make on your own for free. He may think only of his own commission and lead you to extravagantly-priced but poor-quality furnishings.

WHO CAN BE AN INTERIOR DESIGNER?

No matter how confused you are about furniture styles, colors and what goes with what, *you* could go into business today as an interior designer. Anyone at all can claim to be an interior designer. As furniture expert Wallace Nutting points out, "There is no competent authority to pass on the competence of the decorator . . . Anybody can pose as a decorator without a license or an examination. The buyer must guess since he can hardly judge as to the ability of the person into whose hands he falls."

In early 1974 the National Council for Interior Design Qualification began considering the possibility of a law to establish legal qualifications for professional designers. However, any such legislation is a long way off in terms of being enacted on a state-by-state basis.

A recent ad for a home-study course in interior decorating noted, "5 good reasons why you should become an interior decorator: 1. You'll make money. Designing and furnishing even a single room for a client may earn a decorator a fine commission. Doing an entire apartment, or a house, or a professional suite may bring in a real bonanza. . . . 2. You'll have fun. . . . 3. You'll be somebody. . . . Maybe you'll become a celebrity. Many decorators have. . . . 4. Your time is your own. . . . 5. You have a future." Nowhere is any mention made of the student's ability, intelligence or talent, because it is perfectly legal for an individual with only the goals listed in the ad—or even lesser goals—to become a decorator.

While there are pseudo-decorators to beware of, there are, of course, capable, well-trained designers too. How can you find the well-trained designer? First, you can go by recommendation. If you have a friend who has successfully used a designer, call and get the name. Second, you may visit model homes and apartments in your area and note the name of the designer who furnished the interiors. Third, you may contact the

American Society of Interior Designers (see Chapter 10 for address) for the names of designers in your area.

The A.S.I.D. is the national association for professional designers, and membership in it is an indication of training and competence. The society was born in early 1975 as the result of the merger of two long-standing interior design associations—American Institute of Interior Designers and the National Society of Interior Designers.

Before a designer can join this prestigious group he must have had substantial experience in interior design. This experience must consist of a specified blend of academic training and practical experience.

Membership in the A.S.I.D. is an indication of training, but you should not rule out designers who are not members. Many capable designers are not members.

Finally, many department and furniture stores offer decorating services to customers. These services range from excellent to fraudulent. Just because a store bills an individual as a decorator doesn't mean he is one. A retailer may hire a homemaker with a "flair" and crown her the store professional decorator. At other stores decorators are just salesmen with color wheels and tape measures. They will mix and match anything on their showroom floor in order to make a sale. Their training may run the gamut from nonexistent to having read an issue or two of *Better Homes and Gardens*. Be wary of the store that advertises that all of its salespeople are decorators. More likely, none of them really is.

One prestigious suburban store that bills all its salespeople as decorators handles the situation this way. The store carries top-quality furniture only in traditional styles—no modern, no Early American. The idea is that anything in the store goes with anything else. The decorator-salesman will agree to take a persistent customer to manufacturers' showrooms—but only the showrooms of those manufacturers already doing business with the store. The shopper in this store gets the advice of a salesman trained to sell one style of furniture. She does not get a floor plan, showroom service or the "eye" and experience of a real trained decorator.

Don't give up on stores as a source of good decorating services! Some stores hire A.S.I.D. members as decorators; others make sure their decorators are well trained and experienced; still others provide both academic and practical training to outstanding salespeople. Recently, the Interior Design Society was formed to give some status to store decorators who may not qualify for membership in the "big two" professional associations. At the minimum—there are several classes of membership, just as there are in the A.S.I.D.—an individual who has been employed as a decorator-salesperson for two years may be an I.D.S. member.

A big plus for the store decorator is the fact that he is backed by the store's guarantees of service and quality and by the service capabilities of the store. (Of course, this is a plus only if you have chosen a store with good standards of service and quality.) Buy through this decorator and your merchandise will be delivered to the store, unpacked and inspected. Any touch-up required will be taken care of before the merchandise is delivered to you. Also, if the items fail to give the service you expected, you may turn to the store for satisfaction.

In contrast, if you buy through an independent designer, you must pay shipping charges, and merchandise is delivered direct to your home— most often by a cartage company. This means no unpacking, no setup and no inspection prior to delivery.

Delivery delays are a problem for the decorator as well as the retailer. The delays originate at the factory, and the decorator can do no more to speed up the process than the retailer can. However, as Philip Kelley, president of the super-quality furniture firm Baker, Knapp & Tubbs, pointed out during a meeting of designers, not all designers give their customers "honest delivery information." While this sometimes happens because a designer doesn't get honest information from the supplier, more often it is the consequence of his wish to avoid losing the sale.

Whether you turn to an independent, a member of a professional association or a designer employed by a store, you should check on credentials and experience.

WHAT CAN A DESIGNER DO FOR YOU?

Decorators offer a variety of services, and it is up to you to specify the services you need. You may hire a designer to help you do as little as select one chair, curtain one problem window or devise a color scheme. Or you may hire a designer to work with the architect in creating the basic plans for your new home. The designer can oversee structural changes in your home or simply obtain unique accessories for an already-furnished room.

Some designers work strictly as consultants. A design consultant may come to your home for a full day, measure the area to be decorated and provide you with a detailed plan for that room, complete with fabric and color swatches and sources for furnishings. You are given the basic plan and ideas, then you're on your own for the shopping and buying.

You may also use a designer as a buying agent. As mentioned earlier, there are many lines of home furnishings that are sold "to the trade only." That means that you as a private customer may not purchase them, nor are they sold through retail outlets. Such lines are sold only through interior designers. Sometimes standard furniture lines sold through regular retail outlets are offered in special fabrics or finishes to designers only. These "trade only" lines are usually expensive, so if you aren't planning to invest in top-of-the-line furnishings, don't worry about them.

Again, when engaging a designer, you must specify the kind of work you want done. Not all designers offer a range of services. Not all designers will consent to acting as buying agents; not all will work on a piecemeal or small-job basis.

SET UP AN INTERVIEW

The way to find out who will do what is to meet and interview the designer. There is seldom a charge for the initial interview, and this interview is an excellent opportunity not only to obtain definite facts, but to see if you *like* the designer personally. You will be working together on a project that will require mutual respect, understanding and cooperation for the best results.

However, establishing a rapport is not the sole purpose of the interview. You are engaging this individual to do a job for which you will pay. You are entitled to ask questions and to receive straight answers. Don't be intimidated if the designer acts insulted or injured by a sincere or well-justified question. Sandie, a young suburbanite, asked a store decorator, "Where did you study to become a decorator?", and was told, "I prefer to be called a designer." Sandie then asked, "Have you been with this store long?" The designer countered with "Don't you think I can handle the job?" In this case, probably not.

If you are not familiar with the designer's work, ask about his background. Ask to see samples of recent work—these may be rooms in model homes or private homes, or room settings in a store.

Find out if your tastes are compatible. Your home should reflect your interests and preferences, not the designer's. Some designers are well known for their expertise in working with a particular style or period of furniture design. It's foolish to engage a designer renowned for his far-out, prophetic work with modern styles if you long for a cozy, buttons-and-bows Colonial room.

Find out what it is going to cost you. Be absolutely honest about how much you want done and how much you can afford to spend. Tell the designer whether you can spend this sum all at once or whether you must budget it over a period of weeks or months. If he feels your amount or budget is totally out of line, the designer will say so and perhaps direct you to another decorating source.

Honesty is the key to an effective interview. Sometimes a woman is embarrassed to admit to a fashionable designer that she has to work on a budget, and she presents a false picture of her financial situation. Sooner or later she is going to have to pay, and once things are ordered and the project begun, it's far more embarrassing to confess to a lack of funds.

Some women are embarrassed to have the designer come into their homes to see what botches they have made of things on their own. In fact, computer decorating services are being devised just so that these embarrassing situations can be avoided. Of course, just as removal of the personal confrontation eliminates embarrassment, it also eliminates individualized counseling. Generally, the computer confines itself to a run-down of your favorite colors, fabrics and furniture styles. It may inquire as to the dimensions of the room to be decorated and which of your present pieces you plan to incorporate in the new design. Questions related to your personality bear an amazing resemblance to the contrived quizzes discussed in Chapter 3. A few large manufacturers are dabbling in this concept at present because it presents distinct advantages to them: the computer will offer only their merchandise.

WHO CHARGES WHAT AND HOW?

Many people who would like to consult a decorator are afraid to, primarily because of cost. In an article in the Cleveland *Press*, Sherwood Falsgraf, president of A.I.D., was interviewed as follows:

Q. Does the average guy who plans to redo his home even consider going to a designer for help?

FALSGRAF: No.

Q. Why not?

FALSGRAF: I wish I knew. If I did, I'd be a very wealthy man today.

Q. You must have some idea on how to approach that guy?

FALSGRAF: Any attempt A.I.D. or N.S.I.D. has made in the past to attract the average customer has been a dismal failure.

Q. Do you wonder why? Do you have any kind of answer?

FALSGRAF: Yes, of course I do. I think people have a built-in fear of interior designers costing too much.

Designers' fees vary greatly, depending on such things as geographic area, skill and reputation, and there are many methods of levying charge.

A basic source of profit to the designer is the purchase of your furniture. Designers are able to buy directly from manufacturers or through designer showrooms and to pay the wholesale price—about 40 per cent under retail. Now, the most expensive designer may, in turn, bill you for the full list price plus his consultation fee. As top designers will often accept only jobs that are based on a substantial budget and then will purchase only very expensive furnishings, this plan can run into a great deal of money. At the other extreme, a designer may charge as little as 10 per cent over list price—or even just the wholesale price plus a fee for the entire job.

If you were planning to buy this "designer quality" furniture anyway, and would have done so at retail prices, you may well be dollars ahead by using a decorator whose total bill—wholesale cost plus percentage plus fee—is still under the retail cost. In effect, then, you obtain the designer's skill without exceeding the retail price of the furnishings alone.

If, however, you planned to purchase moderately-priced furniture and are swept along into the upper brackets, you may well exceed your budget by thousands. A designer reasonably enough considers each job a test of his reputation—an advertisement for his skills—and, as a result, will want to use the best materials, merchandise and craftsmen available. This attitude is understandable, but costly.

It doesn't take a financial wizard to see that if a designer can get a bigger commission from one firm than another, he will make more money by steering his customers to the money-making source. That may be good business for him and for the manufacturer, but it certainly may not be good for the shopper. Wallace Nutting declares vehemently, "It is a rule, perhaps without exception, that the larger the commission, the more inferior are the goods dealt in."

So know your interior designer and know furniture on your own. If you have a fair idea of furniture construction and costs in your area, you should be able to detect a bum steer.

The fixed fee is another method of billing used by designers. The designer estimates the amount of time involved in the completion of the job and charges a fixed fee for that amount of time. He then sells the furnishings purchased at the same wholesale prices that he pays.

No matter what method of billing is used, it is customary for a designer to ask for an advance retainer, which is usually a percentage of the total estimated cost. This retainer is deducted from the final bill.

The designer is usually paid in installments. A designer's association has stated, "Generally, there is the retainer plus about one-third of the estimated amount paid upon signing the contract, another sum when about 85 per cent of the work is done, leaving approximately 10 per cent for when the job is completed and which should be paid within 10 to 30 days of completion."

Whether you are working with an independent designer or a store designer, it is a good policy to pay for merchandise as it is delivered to you. That way, if the project drags on for months—as it probably will—you will make smaller periodic payments instead of one blockbuster at the end. Pay-as-you-go will work well for both you and your decorator.

Of course, you may arrive at your own individual plan that is agreeable to both you and your designer.

Designers who work for stores are paid on an entirely different basis. The designer is paid by the store—not by you. He may receive a straight salary or a salary plus commission, or he may work on commission only. You can expect the designer who is working on commission only to push expensive merchandise and room groupings, urging you to "Buy it all now to be sure you can get just what you want. We may not be able to get it later, and you can use our monthly payment plan to pay for it."

However, using the decorating service of a quality store may be an example, for once, of getting something for nothing—or darn close to it. Design departments of some stores are staffed by experts who lead the way in decorating trends and whose services you probably could not afford if they were not subsidized by the stores. As explained earlier, however, in other stores the decorators are only salesmen with no special training or skill. It's up to you to check out the store's reputation, examine the model-room settings and interview the designer.

At one time most stores offered decorator services free of charge and with no obligation. Unfortunately, too many customers abused this generosity and went from store to store, having a good time getting free decorating ideas, with no intention of making a purchase. Now it is customary for stores to charge a nominal sum ($25 to $50) that is deducted from the cost of your purchase. If you do not buy anything, you must pay the fee.

SPELL IT ALL OUT

Once you have found, interviewed and decided on a designer with whom you are compatible both personally and financially, you will have to commit yourself to the project. It is often a good idea to have a written contract which spells out exactly what will be done, by when and for how much. A contract should cover the following points: (1) the minimum and maximum to be spent; (2) the services to be rendered—furnishing an entire house or the selection of a few pieces; (3) method of payment—size and timing of installments; (4) who bears the cost of extras—shipping, taxes, touch-ups, etc; (5) beginning and completion dates of the project (This is especially important if you have a specific deadline to meet. For example, you may want to have a home prepared prior to your moving into it. The designer must then work with your moving date in mind.); (6) termination of contract. (If for some reason—dissatisfaction with the designer, financial reverses, divorce, whatever—you wish to terminate the project, you should understand what obligations you have in terms of minimum payments).

That done, you can move on to the fun part of working with a designer. You talk, the designer listens. Charles Sevigny, one of the most expensive and exclusive designers in the world, has said that the most important thing about any house or apartment is that when you walk into it, the people who live there look like they belong there. The way to make sure the room projects your personality—not the decorator's—is to be frank regarding your likes and dislikes, your interests and hobbies. Be honest about your lifestyle: how do you entertain and how often; do you want a "display-only" living room or one that will stand wear and tear? Talk about color preferences and furniture styles. If you have a definite idea in mind, say so. If you meekly go along, with a "whatever you say" attitude, you have no one to blame but yourself if you are unhappy with the result.

It is often very helpful to have your designer meet all the members of the household. Not only can he check out their likes and dislikes, but he can better *sense* the feeling of your home by meeting all its members.

ALTERNATIVE PLANS

If, after all, you find you cannot afford the services of a designer, and your retailer does not offer a decorator service, you do have other sources of decorating advice. Check into local schools that offer interior design courses. Don't limit your search to schools of design. Even junior colleges may offer two-year associate-degree courses. Some schools have set up free decorating services so that design students may obtain practical experience, while other schools may recommend good students to you.

(Of course, if you have the time and inclination, you could take a course in interior decoration at either a local school or one of the clinics offered by many full-service furniture stores. The clinic may be offered at a small charge, or for free if you purchase an established dollar amount of merchandise from the store, or completely free, with no strings. No matter what the charge, expect any store course to be heavy on commercials for the store and brands carried there.)

Finally, you might turn to a friend whose skill and taste in decorating you admire. If all you really need is moral support and confidence in your own decisions, this might work out O.K., but it's loaded with potential problems. Without maintaining a professional basis, you run the risk of losing your friend altogether if you refuse to accept her design plans, if she criticizes your ideas, or if you disagree over color combinations.

On a dollar-and-cents level, your friend may offer her services free of charge, but she will be unable to gain admittance to decorator showrooms and will not be able to obtain a decorator's discount. While her taste may be good, she may lack the training needed to discern good-quality construction and material that will give you top service.

Are you sure that your friend will have your best interests at heart? That may sound cynical, but a salesman at a fine-quality home furnishings store confided that the mistake most women make is "in bringing in a friend for her approval. Here the customer has shopped and shopped until she decides on just the right chair. Color, style and fabric are everything she wants. Then—her confidence deserts her. My reassurances aren't enough. Her husband's aren't enough. She wants her friend to come in and approve her choice. So she brings in the friend, who kills the whole deal. Why? Not because the chair wasn't good enough—but because it was too good. The friend doesn't want her to have better furniture than she has herself. It's jealousy. I've seen it happen time and again—but people would never believe it of their friends."

SIX

Dealing with the Dealer

Before you venture out to confront the psychologically-programmed, decorator-designed display floor, the wiles of the salesman and the trauma of the credit department, you should do your homework. You should know what style you want, what general color, and what price you want to pay. In order to know what questions to ask and what kind of answers to expect, you must also master a few basics about furniture construction and merchandising.

Whether you are shopping for casegoods or upholstered furniture, there are certain terms you should be familiar with. Manufacturers often produce furniture in suites, groups or collections. Even if the store you buy from carries only a portion of a group or collection, you may order other pieces.

A *suite* consists of a limited number of pieces designed for use in a specific room. For example, a bedroom suite may be made up of a dresser, chest, nightstands and headboard. Suites may be part of the larger group or collection. Suites are always priced as a total unit: "Bedroom suite—$999."

A *group* is a large selection of furniture—often a number of suites—for use in bedroom, dining room and living room, and may include occasional pieces. All the pieces within a group are correlated by design and finish.

A *collection* is an abused term and as commonly used is often interchangeable with "group." However, used precisely, it refers to a mixture of upholstered and wood pieces that blend in style or feeling—as a modern collection or French country collection. Woods, finishes and details in a collection may vary, but the "feeling"—formal, informal, rustic, sophisticated—remains consistent throughout a collection.

Manufacturers are pretty good about using these terms appropriately, but retailers advertise such absurdities as "four-piece collection" and "living room group." Generally speaking, you can't tell for sure from a retailer's ad whether an item of furniture is part of an extensive collection, a large group or a motley bunch. The term "room environment," which has been popping up lately, is just an update on the group.

"Stepping up" in sales jargon means moving the customer up the price ladder from the $200 chair she is eyeing to a $250 or $300 chair. The group is one of the favorite means of stepping up a customer. In fact, the heart and soul of furniture merchandising is selling a group or roomful of furniture at one time. The group offers the retailer faster, easier selling, often with a bigger markup than does selling separate pieces.

Most often the sales pitch for a group is built around the fact that you can buy all the pieces in the group at once, with no chance for error in color or style.

This "no-error idea" is the hook for many shoppers. Too many feel insecure about so monumental an effort as putting an entire room together. They believe that the room coordinated by the retailer is far better than any they could create. Somehow it bears the stamp of authority—"This is O.K. because the store set it up." The "smart" merchandiser puts together groups and room settings from individual pieces on the salesfloor; so can you.

If the manufacturer has coordinated a suite for fabric, color, wood and style, you can be fairly confident that these things do, in fact, blend well. However, a retailer may just group items that aren't selling individually, that "go together pretty well," or that combine to make the right total price for the package.

Don't buy a roomful of furniture just because it's an easy out. In fact, some experts at coping with the economy firmly state, "Avoid buying room packages, suites or groups." Consider each item in the group individually on the basis of construction, quality and design. This applies to living room, bedroom or dining room furniture. If you are buying a bedroom or dining room set on sale or at a reduced price, make sure it is a manufacturer's set and not just the retailer's assortment of rejects and leftovers from various manufacturers. In an effort to move old stock, a retailer may piece together a "set" from a couple of similar suites. He may put new, matching hardware on all the pieces for an appearance of uniformity. However, one piece may have a plastic surface, the others may not. The finish is almost certain to vary somewhat. Check each and every piece in the group.

How about the price of the group? Sometimes a group is a better buy than if the individual items in it were priced separately. At other times a dealer inflates the price of a group just because he knows it's hard for you to compare values. Open-stock, individually priced bedroom and dining room pieces often add up to a higher total price than package-priced suites. But not always. This is one area where you must divide to conquer. Consider each piece individually in terms of cost. What would that sofa cost if sold alone? Many times the retailer will price all the items separately, but will take care to see that the total of individual items adds up to more than the group price.

Ask yourself whether you want each item in the group. Are all the pieces of equal quality? Do you want to spend such a large sum all at once?

Pricing is a fine art in home furnishings merchandising. As explained in Chapter 3, prices are often arbitrarily determined by what the item "looks" as if it will sell for. Then there is the psychology of numbers. You know, $9.99 instead of $10, and so on. Merchandising experts know what prices draw a poor response, what price groups lead to bigger step-ups. Considerable research has been done in this area, and retailers price accordingly.

To some extent, then, price is based on psychology as well as value and appearance.

In addition to the normal operating costs, furniture prices may also reflect the costs of spiffs and PM's. *PM* stands for "push money," and *spiff* means the same thing. They are special bonuses—money, prizes, points toward prizes—that salespeople are paid for switching customers to certain items. The spiffed items usually offer the dealer a higher profit than non-spiffed items, or they may just be hard to sell. Spiffing is not unique to the home furnishings industry; it's really big in appliances. And there is nothing illegal about it, although the Federal Trade Commission says it is often a clue to the illegal bait-and-switch tactic. As far as you the customer are concerned, however, spiffs motivate the salesperson to intensify the pressure on you to buy the spiffed item.

BEWARE OF BAIT-AND-SWITCH

Spiffing is legal, but bait-and-switch isn't. The federal government has outlawed this old routine, but it has been around so long and is so much a part of some dealers' way of selling that it will be years before it vanishes altogether. (The fact that so many shoppers continue to fall for it only helps to keep it around.)

Bait-and-switch is used by dealers to sell all kinds of merchandise, not only home furnishings. As expressed by the Federal Trade Commission, the key to bait-and-switch is sincerity. The dealer never sincerely intends to sell the advertised "bait," but plans to "switch" you to other merchandise. In fact, in a bait-and-switch operation the salesman not only gets no commission on the bait, but probably will be reprimanded if it is sold.

According to the FTC, the purpose of bait advertising is "to switch consumers from buying the advertised merchandise, in order to sell something else, usually at a higher price or on a basis more advantageous to the advertiser. The primary aim of a bait advertisement is to obtain leads as to persons interested in buying merchandise of the type so advertised."

You cannot assume that well-known firms will not indulge in this old switcheroo. In the summer of 1974 the Federal Trade Commission issued a complaint against Sears, Roebuck, charging the use of bait-and-switch tactics in selling appliances. (The FTC issues a complaint when it has "reason to believe" that the law has been violated. This action does not imply adjudication of the charges.)

When you take the bait and go to the store looking for a "stunning velvet-covered 90-inch sofa" at a remarkably low price, the salesman will use one or more techniques to switch you to other merchandise. He may ignore your request to see the advertised merchandise and enthusiastically show you other, more expensive or more profitable sofas. Perhaps he'll just tell you the advertised sofa is all sold out, except for the floor sample, and that will be "nailed down," meaning he won't sell it. Another favorite technique is to put down the bait as being beneath you: "This is O.K. for some folks who don't know or want anything better, but I can see that you're accustomed to finer things." Finally, the bait may well be beneath even the most indiscriminate junk man. Shoddy, water-stained, soiled or used merchandise is sometimes presented as the advertised merchandise—and "Of course you don't want that."

If you do find yourself enmeshed in bait-and-switch, beat a hasty retreat. You don't want to do business with this kind of operation. Don't think you're going to insist on the bargain bait and outmaneuver the dealer. If you are persistent enough, he may sell you the bait, and switch you later. He may take your deposit or payment and then fail to deliver— or deliver a defective item. When you protest, you are switched to other merchandise.

SPECIAL ORDERS

Perhaps after shopping at several stores, you still cannot find exactly what you want. You find the right color, but not on the right style of chair; you find the style of breakfront you want, but not in the finish you hoped for; maybe you found the style of sofa you want, but in the wrong length. Special ordering may be the answer. Special ordering is one of the causes of high production and distribution costs in the home furnishings industry; it adds to the delivery delay, but it permits you to obtain precisely what you want to complete your décor.

Special ordering involves a number of possible pitfalls. Policy regarding special orders varies from store to store, so you cannot assume that because you followed one procedure with Store A, it's going to work the same way with Store B. Some stores permit cancellations of special orders; others do not. Some will accept the return of special-order merchandise if you are dissatisfied; others will not. Some stores require a sizable deposit; others demand a much smaller amount.

A dealer who will not accept the return or cancellation of special-order merchandise is not necessarily being uncooperative; he may simply be passing on to you the conditions laid down by the manufacturer. Also, if he does permit you to return the merchandise, it's up to him to try to sell this custom piece. You may have ordered extras or fabric that raise the cost of the item beyond his store's selling range; or you may have ordered such a "unique" item that no one else would even consider it.

If you do place a special order, pay close attention to the sales contract. Read the terms regarding cancellations, returns, guarantees, and payment terms (amount of deposit, when total payment is due). Check the description of the merchandise—style and model number; wood, finish, color; size; quantity; grade of upholstery. If you have to go back to the display area to do this checking, do so. Don't be discouraged by a salesperson anxious to close the sale. If the order is wrong and the item is incorrectly made up as a result, you may be stuck with it. Add up all the extras for the total price—labor charges, shipping, delivery, handling, as well as decorative extras on the item ordered, such as special stain-resistant finishes, casters, arm covers, etc.

You may encounter these abbreviations: FOB—freight on board (a delivery charge); COM—customer's own material (you're supplying the upholstery fabric); COD—cash on delivery; CBD—cash before delivery.

Make sure your copy of the order is clear (triplicate carbons sometimes get pretty faint); note the name of the salesperson.

THE SKINNY-WALLET NINE

"The Consumer Game," a Chicago Public Television show, dramatically outlined "The Skinny-Wallet Nine," nine common sales techniques which "can dramatically reduce the weight of your pocketbook." According to this show, these nine techniques are used anywhere you deal with the professional salesman face to face. You are sure to encounter some or all of them as you shop for home furnishings. They are

1. Identification. A good salesman will sell himself before he sells his product.
2. Negative take-away. A take-away phrase is described as "one in which the salesman implies that he doesn't really want to make the sale unless the prospect positively insists." For example, "I don't want to sell this carpet to you unless I am sure it is absolutely right for your home."
3. Magic words. Words such as "amazing," "guarantee," "truth" have all been proven to have the ability to seduce the customer into buying.
4. "Yes" question. The salesperson asks a series of "yes" questions— "Don't you want to know all you can about this upholstery fabric?" "Don't you intend to let your kids use this sofa?" —to lead you to the next plateau in his pitch.
5. Commitment question. As defined (not altogether grammatically) in the television show, "This is an attempt to get a positive commitment from the prospect that they definitely do want the product if they could afford it." It translates in action into questions like "If price were no object, is this the mattress you would want?"
6. Verbal proof story. Called the single most successful sales technique, the verbal proof story makes it appear that some completely

objective third party—not the salesman—is endorsing the product. "I just wish Fred Jones was here now. He bought a mattress like this one a few months ago and says he has no more backaches and sleeps like a baby."

7. Double positive. Rather than ask if you want to buy, the salesperson assumes the sale and simply gives you two positive choices, "Which would look better in your living room? The gold velvet or the blue tweed?"

8. Now factor. For some reason—"This is the last one in stock, I wouldn't delay." "I don't know how long this special price is good for. Tomorrow the price could be up."—tomorrow will be too late to buy. The salesperson is pushing for an immediate commitment.

9. Blowup and drop. The salesperson sets up an inflated price and, if you don't jump for it, drops to another item at a lower price.

CASEGOODS

The term "casegoods" applies to non-upholstered furniture, such as tables, breakfronts, dressers and chests. With little care, good-quality casegoods will give service and beauty to your home for many years. Poor-quality casegoods offer little beauty and may warp, crack and split, and generally will look lousy in a very short time. It's worth your time and effort to learn something about woods, plastics, finishes and casegoods construction before you spend your money.

Basically, there are two kinds of wood casegoods—solid and veneer. Years ago veneer was sneered at as being just a thin sheet of wood glued to a piece of solid lumber. However, the sneering is over. Veneered furniture is now considered better than solid furniture in many respects, and 90 per cent of today's furniture is veneered.

A veneer is a wood sandwich usually made up of five to seven thin layers bonded together. The more layers, the better. The core of the sandwich should be a solid piece of wood. (Check this. If it's some composition or pressed-board variety, it may warp with time. A hang-tag should detail materials used—if no tag is on item, ask to see the manufacturer's catalog sheet.) On each side of this core, a thin sheet of strong hardwood is placed at cross-grain to it. A face or front veneer of fine cabinet wood and a back veneer are placed over the cross-band layers—again at cross-grain. All of the layers are held together with strong adhesives and are bonded under heat and pressure. The result is stronger—pound for pound—than steel and certainly stronger than a solid board of the same thickness.

In addition to strength, veneering has other advantages. It is highly resistant to warping, changes in temperature, humidity, airconditioning and overheating. Veneered furniture is also less costly than solid wood because the expensive cabinet woods are used only on the face layer. Veneer is attractive to the manufacturer because it can be readily bent and molded to almost any curve desired; drum forms and the curved edge of a grand piano are good examples of the workability of veneer. So if a well-intentioned grandmother tells you that veneer is really a poor second in quality to solid wood, you know better.

Solid wood furniture is made of planks of wood at least one-half to three-quarters of an inch thick, and all exposed parts of the piece are solid lumber. Whether an item is veneered or solid, however, all legs or supporting parts should be of solid wood.

There are two main categories of furniture woods—softwood and hardwood. Softwood comes from the needle-bearing, evergreen trees; hardwoods from leaf-bearing trees. Softwoods, such as pine, are generally used only in Early American, rustic or unfinished furniture. The hardwoods are more commonly used and are the most beautiful. Birch, maple, mahogany, cherry, oak, walnut, and teak are some of the most popular hardwoods in use today. They may be used alone or in combination with more exotic woods such as ebony, rosewood, and myrtle. When the term "fine cabinetwood" is used, hardwoods are being discussed. (Note: Fruitwood is a kind of hardwood that comes from fruit-bearing trees. Very often, however, the term "fruitwood" is used to describe the finish, so that you may find a fruitwood finish on, for example, pecan.)

Any of these woods may be used to produce a beautiful, strong and long-lasting piece of furniture. If you wish to obtain information on a specific wood you may write to the Fine Hardwoods Association (see Chapter 10 for address).

That a piece of furniture is made of hardwood, however, is not a guarantee of quality. You must consider the grade of hardwood and the way in which it is used. Hardwoods may be cut to display various figures and grains in the wood. A portion of the price you pay should reflect the degree of care used in matching grain, shading and pattern.

No matter how tight your budget, when you are contemplating the purchase of casegoods, check out the top-quality pieces first to see what fine cabinetry looks like. Look at the wood—the veneering, the grain, the finish, the color of the woods used—run your hand over it, feel it, thump it. You may decide to sacrifice size, number of pieces or fancy hardware in exchange for really fine wood craftsmanship within your financial limits.

The finishing touch

Whatever the wood, its finish should both enchance and protect it. At one time when you talked about furniture finishes, you were talking about varnish. No more. Varnish has been almost totally eclipsed by oil finishes and the "super" finishes that offer protection as well as beauty. An oil finish gives a dry, matte glow to the wood and is most often seen on modern pieces of teak, walnut, and rosewood. The chemically-created "super" finishes render wood surfaces highly resistant to scratches, mars, even cigarette burns—without distorting the natural beauty of the wood itself.

A distressed finish refers to scratches, marks, wormholes, specks that are deliberately created to produce an antique look. Distressed pieces are beaten with metal chains by the manufacturer—not as some act of perversion, but to blunt corners, soften edges and create an appearance of wear. Distressed pieces may also feature mar-proof tops.

Painted finishes in a whole spectrum of colors from pale pastels to patriotic red, white and blue wax and wane in popularity. A painted finish may also feature distressed touches and touches of gold—both adding to the cost. Certainly a good painted finish adds to the cost of a piece of furniture, and a poorly-done paint job screams "cheap" all the way across the room.

Whatever finish you choose, it should be perfectly matched on all surfaces. The top—whether solid wood or a laminated plastic—should blend with the rest of the piece. There should be no drips, runs, streaks or deposits of the finishing material. The texture of the surface, too, should be evenly smooth throughout, with no ripples, bubbles or irregularities. Last-minute factory touch-ups are a common irritation to be watched for.

When checking the finish on a dining table, be sure to compare the leaves to the table. They should, of course, be a perfect match.

Plastic furniture of the future today

The lovely finish of perfectly-matched grain may not be wood at all. Research has produced plastics of a wide variety, some so like wood in both texture and appearance that it is difficult to detect the difference.

Furniture may be all or part plastic. Vinyl veneers may be applied somewhat like wood veneers; in fact, some vinyl veneers may include a thin layer of real wood. These veneers are made up of three layers: the top is a transparent vinyl that protects against damage; the second layer is wood veneer; and the third is aluminum foil for heat resistance. Other vinyl veneers simulate wood graining through a photographic process. A photographic image of wood—any color, any wood— is covered with a vinyl film and, with adhesives and high pressure, is laminated to unfinished furniture surfaces. The unfinished core of such pieces is certainly not quality hardwood, but most likely particle board, flakeboard, or what is called "core stock."

Plastics are found not only on furniture tops, but also are in use as carvings and decorative panels. The heavy, ornate carving so prevalent in Mediterranean styles is often achieved through the use of "molded components" made by pouring plastic into design molds. The finished panel is applied to the piece of furniture.

Obviously, then, what appears to be a solid wood dresser may well be core stock wrapped with vinyl and decorated with molded plastic panels. It's not always easy to detect. Plastic parts have been reinforced to pass the "thump" test. New glazing processes give plastics a visual depth never before possible.

Plastics are a big part of the market and are getting bigger all the time. By 1985 the furniture industry is expected to consume four billion pounds of plastic per year. Clearly, as a shopper you will have to be able to recognize plastic when you meet it—and you're going to meet it more often. It seems fair to say that you will be pretty much on your own, too, at identifying and evaluating plastic and its use in the item you are considering. Salesmen are most often reluctant to discuss it.

You may have noticed that no matter how technologically terrific the advances regarding plastic are, retailers always avoid using the word "plastic." They chatter about "wood-look," "high-pressure surfaces," "molded panels," but never plastic. To most people, furniture is wood. *Plastic World*, a plastics-trade magazine, has stated that "between 80 and 90 per cent of the retail market favors traditional materials and designs." That means wood over plastic.

The very word "plastic" has come to have bad connotations. It has, in fact, become a general putdown about almost anything—"The suburbs are so plastic"; "Everything about Las Vegas is so plastic"; "She's so phony—a really plastic personality." Used this way, plastic is equated with inferior and cheap. Well . . . is it?

It is certainly cheaper to turn out molded plastic panels than to hire a craftsman to carve the same design in wood. Advocates of plastic as a substitute for wood point out that polyurethane was responsible for the popularity of Spanish- and Mediterranean-style furniture, as it brought it within the price range of the masses. Charles S. Shaughnessy, Jr., vice president, casegoods sales of Singer Company, pointed out, "Without plastic moldings, door and drawer components and detailed design ornamentation, the average American consumer would not be able to afford most furniture in designs that are a translation of past periods or heritages that she wants." Vinyl veneer wraps can be laminated to low-cost particle board to produce durable casegoods at rock-bottom prices. In an effort to keep material and production costs low, much plastic furniture is mass produced with a vengeance. If you care about being exclusive, it isn't for you.

Low price is a big factor in favor of choosing plastic or part-plastic furniture, but the best-designed, best-quality plastic pieces may be surprisingly costly. Plastic raw materials are sold by the pound, and heavier or thicker plastic is usually of better quality—with accompanying higher cost. Better plastic pieces will equal the cost of some good-quality all-wood pieces and exceed the cost of inexpensive wood furniture. Plastic doesn't mean low cost.

A furniture retailer in Saginaw, Michigan, headlined an ad for bedroom suites: "Plastic is for Ping-Pong balls . . . not for fine furniture!" Is he right? Is plastic an inferior substitute for wood? Well . . . yes and no. Aesthetically, wood-look plastics just don't measure up to the look of real wood. They don't have the highlights, depth, richness, luster or patina of wood. Plastics will not mellow with age. Of course, cheap wood doesn't have any of these qualities either.

Too often plastic components are poorly mated with wood. For example, carved panels may not match the wood base in shade of finish or in texture. They may look simply "stuck on" rather than like an integral part of the piece. The color and texture of molded plastic or vinyl veneers are, generally speaking, uniform throughout. In real wood, they are not.

To be fair, this uniformity may have advantages. John Harmon, vice president, Basic-Witz Corporation, enthusiastically stated, "A furniture manufacturer can make his mold with the most superb grain characteristics and definition he can find, and every piece of furniture made from that mold is just as lovely as the original." It's a lot like plastic flowers versus fresh flowers. The plastics never fade, wither or die; they don't have bugs or thorns. But they never look as good as the real thing either.

So far all the discussion of plastics in furniture has been about plastic traveling incognito—as wood. Well, plastic has begun to come of age as a furniture material in its own right. It has moved in off the sundeck and into the living room. Much of what is said later regarding strength, durability and maintenance will apply to both wood-look plastic and up-front, plastic-look plastic. Aesthetically, however, there is a difference.

All-wood furniture may be had in styles ranging from ultratraditional to ultramodern, but so far plastic-as-plastic furniture is usually used only in far-out modern in bright, slick colors. Imaginative, innovative designs are prevalent in the better plastic-look lines. Injection-molded; cantilevered design; curvilinear—these are descriptive terms so often applied to this furniture.

Plastic-as-plastic furniture is found in all furniture categories, for all rooms. It makes no excuses for being plastic. It doesn't pretend to be anything else—and, while it may appear youthful, witty and casual, will give your home all the warmth and coziness of an airport waiting room.

How about strength and durability? It all depends upon the plastic and how and where it is used. Some plastics are virtually indestructible; others, easily scratched or cracked. Plastic legs on casegoods may well be brittle and require reinforcement of steel or wood. Occasionally the reinforcement material places stress on the plastic during temperature change, resulting in splitting and cracking. Splitting and cracking, in fact, are the biggest problems with plastic. Laminated tops, if not properly done, will split from the base at the edges; a sharp instrument can scratch plastic surfaces; hollow molded panels can be punctured. While wood that is damaged may be repaired by sanding, filling or refinishing, damaged plastic is usually beyond help.

Chemicals and abrasive cleaners are deadly on most plastic finishes— but, then, they are not recommended for wood either. The same holds true for strong, direct heat; certain plastics melt, char or burn in response to such heat. However, a dropped cigarette or boiling liquid will not have any effect unless the heat is prolonged, so under ordinary household conditions this shouldn't present a problem.

Plastic finishes are not totally maintenance-free. A wipe with a damp cloth or with a liquid detergent is sufficient. Because traditional furniture waxes just gum up on plastic surfaces, some manufacturers recommend a good automobile paste wax for use on plastic furniture. It is seldom mentioned that although plastic furniture is easy to care for, you may have to care for it more often. Louis Bolling, owner of a Manhattan furniture store, says, "Some of this type of merchandise looks fine when it's new, but even though it gets no more than the normal abuse furniture receives in a busy store, it requires frequent dusting and buffing." Static build-up on some plastics tends to hold dust—a less than winning trait.

When one major producer of middle-price casegoods turned from "all wood" products to wood with plastic panels, a spokesman for the firm said, "It may not be the same suite to us and our dealers, but it is to the consumer and it's something she can afford." It shouldn't be the same thing to the consumer either. There are differences between plastic and wood, and any shopper should be aware of them before she buys.

There are enough different plastics to boggle the mind of a chemist. Thankfully, they are not all used in furniture; only about a dozen are. The two major classifications for all plastics are thermoplastics and thermoset plastics.

Thermoplastics, in theory, can be melted down and re-formed. This is the group that can be damaged by being subjected to strong, sustained heat. Thermoset plastics pass through a chemical change that hardens them so that they cannot be returned to a liquid state when heated.

In the early 1970's state and federal governments began to take an active interest in establishing standards regarding the flammability of home furnishings products. There is strong concern that some plastics may, in fact, be a real fire hazard—they may cause fire to spread rapidly, ignite in a flash, produce dense or toxic smoke. You may wish to contact the Society of the Plastics Industry, Inc. (see Chapter 10 for address) for up-to-date information on plastics as fire hazards.

Thermoplastics
ABS plastic   ABS stands for Acrylonitrile-Butadiene-Styrene and is known under the brand name Cycolac—all of which calls up images of computers, robots and laboratories, not sofas, tables or living rooms. It's tough enough to use for football helmets and is weather resistant. Its glossy, opaque surface can be kept clean with mild soap and a damp cloth, polished with auto wax . . . or toothpaste. Don't use powdered cleansers, abrasives, brushes; ABS scratches. Like all thermoplastics, ABS will soften or melt under heat, but that heat has to be above 175 to 212

degrees. You'll find ABS used for tables, chairs, and all kinds of avant-garde pieces.

Acrylic   Acrylics, formally known as polymethylmethacrylate, scratch and cloud up like crazy. Sliding a coaster across an acrylic table top will leave a trail of hairline scratches. Acrylic is structurally stronger than glass, but will crack if hit sharply. It melts and distorts under flame—so watch out for direct heat. Known under such brand names as Lucite, Plexiglas and Acrylite, this plastic may be transparent, opaline, translucent, or opaque; colored or clear. It gets pretty expensive—especially clear acrylic.

Polystyrene   Polystyrene masquerades as wood with great success. You'll find it used on furniture surfaces as arms, legs and headboards, and as simulated wood carvings. It may have either a smooth or textured surface that can be readily cleaned with a damp cloth and mild soap. Like other plastics, polystyrene shouldn't be cleaned with abrasives or cleaning fluids. The surface is tough and will resist damage from most household liquids—except nail polish and nail-polish remover.

Polyolefins   The polyolefins turn up in use as waste baskets, hampers, wine racks and low-quality furniture. You can wipe this plastic clean with a damp cloth, but you'll do it often because it builds up a static charge and holds dust. It may look like wood at a distance, but not up close.

Thermoset plastics
Polyurethane   Polyurethane may be either rigid or flexible. When flexible, it's used for cushioning; when rigid, it's used for simulated-wood decoration. It's tough and is remarkably resistant to household chemicals. You'll come across it as simulated-wood decoration, in lamp bases and in some limited structural use. There are few reports on its long-range effectiveness as structural material.

Polyester   Polyester may be transparent, translucent or opaque; when well-molded, it can be a real fooler as a wood look-alike. It's brittle—more so than ABS or polystyrene—and needs reinforcement for use as tables or chairs. Used alone it is most effective as decorative trim, panels and frames.

Melamine   Melamine is the plastic that is laminated to flat surfaces to produce the popular no-mar tops on dressers, tables, and desks. Formica is a big brand name among the melamines. Laminated to plywood, a clear melamine top will give you the *look* of wood with the toughness of plastic.

To sum up plastics: they can be better in some situations than wood and worse in others. Plastics may bring a particular style down in cost so as to make it affordable in the medium-price market. For the ecology-minded, plastics, though not recyclable, save on trees. Plastic surfaces are super in kid's rooms, family rooms—anywhere that furniture is subjected to rugged treatment. Remember, though: plastics are man-made. You can't expect miracles from them. They will scratch, crack, melt, split and dent. Poorly-applied plastic components and surfaces are a blight to the eye.

Since many salesmen don't even know the difference between mahogany and pecan, you don't stand a very good chance of getting a salesman to identify a specific plastic. Hang-tags, however, may specify the kind of plastic used.

The FTC strikes again

Regardless of what you choose—wood or plastics, solid or veneer construction, hardwood or soft—be sure that's what you get. In December 1973, over the heart-rending wails of furniture dealers, the Federal Trade Commission promulgated *Guides for the Household Furniture Industry* to help the consumer sort out technological marvels from the real thing. Now retailers cannot advertise "the look of decorator-favored pecan" or "the rich, warm glow of walnut," unless the items in question are actually pecan or walnut. Too often a walnut painted finish was mistaken by shoppers for the real thing . . . and the retailers encouraged the buyer to make that mistake. The luxurious-sounding phrase "rich sculptural effects" may no longer be used to describe molded plastic components. The description must now read "carved effects of simulated wood." Painted finishes, veneers, simulated wood, leather or marble and molded components must all be clearly identified as such.

The rulings also extend to style. Furniture cannot be described as Danish when, in fact, it was made in Hoboken, New Jersey. Instead, such terms as "Danish style" or "Spanish influence" must be employed to describe a furniture style.

The FTC rules apply to hang-tags too. However, instead of producing hang-tags with full information on furniture construction, materials and finishes, some manufacturers reacted to the rulings by eliminating information. As expressed by Philip Kelley, president of Baker, Knapp & Tubbs, a firm that markets very expensive, top-quality furniture: ". . . it would appear that the more you say, the more trouble you are in." Therefore, Kelley says, "We're not going to put more on our tags than we have to. So you don't have to spend half the day explaining it to the consumer."

Giving less information instead of running the risk of violating the FTC guidelines is also a strategy used in ads. Ralph Nader, in a speech to the Retail Advertising Conference on home furnishings advertising and the FTC standards, said, "Advertisers are now liable to make the more vague assertion which conveys a mood and sense of confidence in the product, rather than conveying the specific standard of comparison that is really a far more acceptable way for retailers to advertise."

Certainly, if it is possible for advertisers to avoid being misleading by simply giving the minimum amount of information, the FTC rules will not end your obligation to protect yourself. It is up to you to read ads carefully, discern what is missing and ask about it. ASK—don't assume anything. Be aware that "the look of walnut" is just that—only the look, the finish. Don't stop there; find out what is being finished.

Built to last

After you've walked your legs off to the knees looking for just the "right" breakfront—a terrific style at the right price—it's tempting to have the order written up instantly. Wait a minute. Look beyond that terrific style for some basic construction features. It sounds dull and tiresome, but, if poorly constructed, that "just-what-I-want" breakfront will turn into just-what-you-don't-want—a warping, splitting wreck.

Construction features on casegoods are easy to examine. In fact, they are often deliberately made a design feature. When checking the construction of any casegoods item, forget about your dignity. If you have to get down on your hands and knees to check joints and fastenings, do it. Pull out drawers, open doors—get active!

What do you look for? Well, let's divide casegoods into all-plastic and wood categories. The construction guidelines for each are quite different.

Plastic

Heavy gauge or thickness in plastics is usually an indication of better quality, according to Vaungarde, Incorporated, an award-winning manufacturer of plastic furniture. The edges of plastic furniture should be smooth (none of those sharp edges or little wisps to show the mold line). The surface should be flawless—no bubbles or ripples. Color should be even throughout. The best pieces should be finished on all sides.

Wood

Instinctively, it seems, shoppers test casegoods' construction by first giving an item a good shove to see if it wobbles. Experts also tell you to make the wobble test. Well, that's right. Your casegoods shouldn't wobble; but before you dismiss a piece as poorly constructed, check out the floor it's sitting on. An uneven floor can make even the finest furniture rock.

Joints   Joints are the key to the strength and sturdiness of wood furniture. In furniture construction two pieces of wood are fitted together to form what is called a "joint." The joints are the key to the strength and sturdiness of wood furniture, and you should check them.

There are several kinds of joints, but all use glue to hold them together. Screws, with washers to prevent wearing of the wood, may be added for extra strength. The joints you are most likely to encounter are the following:

The *dowel joint* is the joint most commonly used in furniture construction. A dowel is a wooden peg which, after being coated with glue, is inserted into aligning holes on opposing pieces of wood.

The *mortise-and-tenon* is another interlocking joint, in which a square or rectangular slot is cut into one piece, and a projecting tongue of wood (the tenon) is shaped on the other. Table tops are often made by joining several boards together by the tongue-and-groove method. (Few table tops are made of one piece of wood. First, it's too difficult to find one piece of wood large enough and good enough to use and, second, such a large piece would be likely to split or warp.)

The *dovetail joint* is made by notching the pieces of wood so that they interlock tightly. A very strong and attractive joint, it is occasionally used decoratively on casegoods' surfaces as part of the design. Dovetailing is often used to join the sides and backs of drawers.

The *butt joint* is easy and cheap to do; it is also the weakest method of

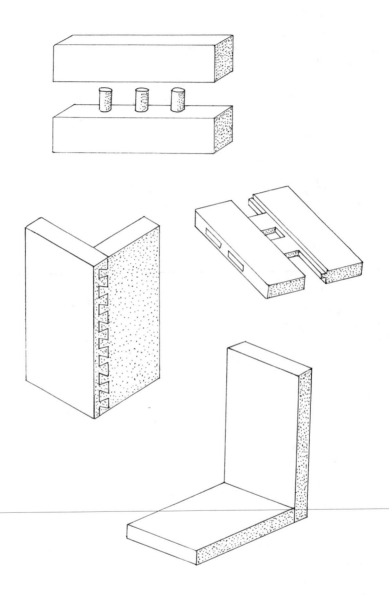

Four common joints used in furniture construction (top to bottom, left to right): dowel joint; dovetailing; mortise and tenon; and butt joint.

joinery. This joint is made by simply butting two pieces of wood against each other without any special grooves or fitting.

Corner blocks or braces are often glued into well-made furniture for added strength at the points of greatest strain.

No matter what kind of joint is used, there should be no gaps or misalignment. Temperature and humidity will, of course, cause a certain *minimal* amount of contraction or expansion of wood, and joints may not always be absolutely perfect.

Drawers offer several indications of the quality of construction, and they are easy to check. Look at the drawers' joints. A well-made drawer will feature dovetailing to join the sides to the front and back. The bottom of the drawer in top-quality furniture will probably be set into grooves cut in the sides, front and back. If the whole drawer is just butted together and tacked, that's a sharp warning as to the construction of the rest of the piece. Look out!

The bottom of a well-made drawer should be blocked at the corners for added support. Look for the guides that will keep the drawer centered and sliding in and out smoothly. These guides may be grooved board, metal, nylon, or plastic slides fastened to the drawer bottom or sides.

The drawer should be sanded smooth on all surfaces. The finest furniture may be finished—waxed or oiled—on the inside. Of course, the drawer will not be made of the same wood as the exposed surfaces. It will probably be made of plywood—in less expensive furniture, of particle board, plastic or cardboard.

More and more frequently drawers are being molded of plastic joined to wood or plastic fronts, and the traditional construction standards, of course, must be abandoned. You aren't going to learn anything about wood construction from a plastic drawer—not even price. As the cost of hand-craftsmanship goes up, more and more furniture manufacturers have turned to plastic drawers. If you are considering a piece with plastic drawers, remember that drawers usually get heavy use. If a plastic drawer is dropped and cracks or splits, there is no practical way to fix it. If the drawers are removed and stacked up during moving, watch out for cracking.

While the drawer is out, look inside the compartment. You will see reinforcement blocks along the sides, a center guide (or, less often, side guides) and dust panels in well-made casegoods. The dust panel is a board which keeps out dust and prevents articles of one drawer from falling into or getting caught in another.

Now slide the drawer back in. Does it glide smoothly? If it binds, balks or sticks, it has been improperly made. Jiggle it from side to side and up and down. The drawer should not rattle around in its compartment, but should fit snugly. Don't let a salesman sell you the story that the drawer is behaving badly just because it's empty: "When you have all your nice things in there, that drawer will just slide in and out perfectly. It's made to work best when filled." Rot—if it sticks or rattles when empty, it's going to be even worse when filled.

When the drawer is closed, check the clearance space around it. The space should be the same width all around—no gap on one side and a tight fit on the other. All the drawers should line up with one another; all hardware should align. Doors on casegoods should also open and close easily, hang properly and fit the opening with no gaps. Two or three hinges are usually used; they should be invisible from the outside of the piece unless purposely exposed for decorative effect. Two friction or magnetic catches are best, and they should be properly placed to hold the door closed. Look at the edge of the door to see if it is veneered or solid. If it is veneered, make sure the edges are neatly finished with a banding strip. The inside of the doors should be veneered and finished, as should the inside of the cabinet.

Decorative molding on door or drawer fronts may well be molded plastic. If so, it should be joined to the base smoothly, with no gaps, edges or glue lines visible. The finish of the molding should, of course, match the rest of the piece perfectly.

Look at the back of the piece. Dressers, buffets, chests that are made to stand against the wall will not be finished on the back. However, the back should be of hardwood or plywood—not composition board or, worst of all, cardboard. The back should be set into grooves, glued and screwed to the frame. It should not be simply nailed on and should never be stapled.

Hardware   If you don't like the decorative hardware—handles and knobs—on a piece, ask if it can be changed. The dealer can sometimes do this. As a general rule, the heavier the hardware, the better. Cheaper hardware is usually stamped, so the metal is much thinner than that used for cast fittings. If a piece has drop handles, heft one—feel the weight.

Knobs and handles that are meant to be used—not to serve as mere decoration—should be properly sized. That is, inset handles should be deep enough for you to get your fingers into without breaking off your nails. Knobs should be large enough to get a grip on. Hardware should be well finished—no sharp edges, no garish painted look.

All fittings should be aligned on each drawer, and each drawer should align with all others. Generally, handles should be screwed on, and the screws should go all the way through the drawer front. Tacked-on or nailed-on handles are likely to pull off in time.

Wood chairs and occasional pieces   Wood chairs, such as those used in the dining room, have a few special construction considerations. After all, unlike a cocktail table, that chair is going to bear a considerable amount of weight. Be sure any wood chair you are planning to buy has corner-block construction. Stretchers—rails that connect the legs on the back and sides and sometimes the front too—will add stability. Sit on the chair; lean back, rock from side to side. If the chair feels shaky now, you can be sure it will get worse as time passes. Legs, back splats and finials should be securely joined. Run your hand around the bottom edge of the chair seat. The surface should be smoothly finished.

There is wood furniture designed for every room in the house. In the living room occasional tables, étagères, bookcases, and console chests can all add to the charm of the room while providing practical storage space too—something to remember if you are in tight quarters. Put those decorative pieces to work.

Occasional tables are often used as "leaders"—"Your choice. Three Early American tables for $99." Manufacturers produce what are classed as "promotional" (synonymous with cheap) tables to serve as "starters." You see the ad for the low-cost three-piece group and go to the store where the salesman *starts* you on these tables, but hopes to quickly move you up the price ladder to a more expensive group.

Try not to shop for your occasional tables as a group. You may prefer that they match in style and wood, but if you consider each table on its own merits you will undoubtedly make a better investment.

Decoratively speaking, too, there is no rule stating that you must have three tables—one cocktail and two end tables—in your living room. How about cubes, stacking tables, or benches for a bit more flexibility and variety?

Don't think size dictates price in occasional tables—or any other furniture, for that matter. Some retailers have found, to their delight, that consumers were willing to pay more for the massive Mediterranean-styled furniture simply because it was big. If the table had a storage compartment, the price was, again, easy to raise. Check construction and material quality—not size—as guidelines to price.

If you must make a sacrifice in quality construction for price, lower your standards for the table legs, not the top. You can get strong, well-joined, but inexpensively-made dowel-rod-type legs on a well-finished, nicely-grained top. The top will get most of the attention and wear, and you can be sure a table top with a dull finish, nondescript graining, or bad veneering will be painfully conspicuous.

Glass- or mirror-topped occasional tables can add sparkle, dash and an element of danger to your living room. A dropped cigarette lighter, a glass that slips from your hand, a falling child—they can shatter a glass top with disastrous results. If you decide on a glass-topped table, don't cut costs by getting thin glass. Plate glass one-half to three-quarters inch thick will cost a bit more than thinner glass, but will be worth it in terms of safety and durability.

Acrylic table tops will not shatter or break as readily as glass, but they scratch terribly and you'll spend your life cleaning off fingerprints and dust. They are a real maintenance problem.

Dining rooms

The dining room is most often the room furnished when people "have the money," as dining room furniture is not seen as a vital necessity. However, when they do get around to buying dining room furniture, their main concern is quality. Unless there is no eating space in the kitchen, the dining room is usually reserved for guests—for special-occasion entertaining.

Although the construction guidelines for wood furniture in general hold true for dining room furniture, there are a few special items to watch out for. The dining room table, for example, may expand in one way or another. If it expands with the addition of leaves, find out if the table leaves are included in the price quoted for the table. Open the table right there in the store—just as though you were at home. It should unlock easily and open without the aid of a strong man. Add the leaves yourself, without help. You will at home. See if the leaves fit properly. Do they match the table's finish and grain?

A table may expand by raising a hinged section supported by an extra leg or brace. Make sure this leg has a good lock—you wouldn't want that section of the table to collapse and send your dinner crashing to the floor. No matter how the table expands, check the hardware. Hinges, locks, slides and supports should all be of good quality and easy to operate.

A dining room table must be stable. With the table on an even, level floor surface, lean on it and try to rock from side to side. It shouldn't move or sway. (A pedestal table needs a wide base to avoid rocking.) Check the underside for good joining and corner blocks. Run your hand around the underside of the apron (the strip of wood that supports the top and joins the legs) to be sure it has been smoothly finished. If not, it will snag clothing.

Finally, sit in the chair you plan to use and draw it up to the table. How's the knee clearance? This is particularly important to check if the table and chairs are not a matched set.

At one time dining room sets were designed for full-sized dining rooms and were simply too big for many new homes and apartments. Now, in response to the growing number of apartment and condominium dwellers, manufacturers are turning out "apartment-sized" dining-room sets. You can get buffets, breakfronts, tables, servers and chairs in any style, all scaled down to fit a small dining area.

If you are really cramped for space in your dining room—or don't have a dining room at all—you might find an extension table that pulls out of a desk or buffet useful. The closed unit is no deeper than a standard buffet, but the table frame draws out to an amazing length. Leaves, which may be stored in the unit base, are then added to form the table top.

There are several kinds of storage pieces designed for dining room use. You may, of course, decide that you neither need nor want any of them. You don't have to buy a full dining room set—even if the retailer prices all the pieces as one package. (You don't even have to buy the table and chairs as a unit if you don't want to.) Decide what you want and get a price breakdown on only those pieces.

Think about getting a wall unit for storage in the dining room now and perhaps for housing a sound system in the family room later.

The buffet is a chest-type piece that stands against the wall and is usually table height. The buffet may also serve as the base for an open storage unit called the hutch. The hutch may also be referred to as a "china." A one-piece unit combining a buffet base and open or glass-doored top is also popularly called a "china" or "breakfront," although the term "breakfront" is properly applied only to such a cabinet in which the center section projects forward.

A server is a small piece that often features a flip-top to offer a wide area for serving pieces. This is one top that should definitely be protected by a plastic heat-resistant surface. Don't confuse the all-wood, heavy server with a serving cart—even if the server comes with casters. When the storage compartments are loaded, glasses are on the shelves and serving pieces are on the top, you aren't going to roll this piece anywhere. It's like a refrigerator with casters—it *can* be moved, but seldom is.

Bedrooms   Furnishing the bedroom has more romantic, sexual and emotional overtones than the furnishing of any other room. Ads for bedroom sets abound with such phrases as "Subtle Spanish styling blends warmth with romantic design" and "Provocative curves, a glorious sweep of headboard, a never-ending play of light and shadow against shaped drawer fronts . . . the essence of French styling." Is it any wonder brides buy bedroom furniture first?

Psychiatrists also promote the idea of the well-furnished bedroom. Psychiatrist Ed Guy was quoted in *New York* magazine as saying, "When a couple complains that they can't decorate the bedroom, invariably it's a sign that they're having trouble with the marriage. And when they finally get around to decorating it—even if they're still not the perfect couple— it seems to be a sign that they're planning to stick it out."

If they try to stick it out and still the marriage fails, it might have helped if they had bought a good bedroom set. A publicity release for Baker Furniture Company, Incorporated, faces the problem of divorce as follows: "Still, some marriages don't last a lifetime anymore, and there are occasionally some bitter battles over who gets a Baker bed. Putting up one for auction at Sotheby Parke Bernet to settle the property is 'kinda sad,' says one sentimentalist employee there. But he brightens quickly at the thought that 'a Baker four-poster always brings a good price. That ought to be some consolation.' "

A bedroom set is hardly likely to have any enduring effect on the quality of romance, sex, marriage or even divorce. If you happen to find a bedroom set that really turns you on . . . well, O.K. As the saying goes, "Different strokes for different folks." For most of us, however, a bedroom set is just furniture and should be judged as such.

So, when you're reading those enticing ads for bedroom sets, eliminate the amorous adjectives and concentrate on the number of pieces offered for the total price, the wood and finish used, the style and the sizes.

Bedroom furniture is most often advertised and displayed as a *set*. The set usually consists of a dresser, chest, headboard and mirror, with the nightstands extra. Please note: you do not get a *bed*—only the headboard and, perhaps, footboard. The metal side rails may be extra, and the mattress and foundation certainly are. Brackets to attach the mirror to the dresser are also extra.

When reading ads for bedroom sets, follow the advice given in Chapter 4. Carefully compare the text of the ad with the picture. Don't assume the items pictured are those you get for the advertised package price.

Of course, you need not buy a set of bedroom furniture at all. You may choose to buy storage pieces which can be used anywhere in the home, such as modular wall units and campaign chests, to combine with a mattress and foundation on a simple metal frame. Or you might buy only one or two pieces, such as a headboard and dresser, from a group.

Interior designers report many of their clients are willing to spend great sums on their living room and dining room furniture, but skimp on the bedroom. The reasoning seems to be that the first two are "display" areas, and the bedroom is not.

While you don't have to buy the most expensive designed bedroom furniture, don't buy the cheapest furniture for the bedroom either, simply because it will not be seen. If you must cut back on costs, buy fewer pieces, but do buy the best you can.

Keep mobility in mind when choosing bedroom furniture. Massive dressers and chests as well as super-sized beds may be attractive, but they are difficult to move and require generously-sized bedrooms. Such large bedroom furniture will also narrow your choice of homes when you do move.

Headboards are bought by size. To choose the right size headboard you must know what size mattress you will be using (see Chapter 7). Headboard widths are designated by the following: 3/3—3 feet, 3 inches, or twin size; 4/6—4 feet, 6 inches, or standard double; 5/0—5 feet, or queen size; 6/6—6 feet, 6 inches, or king size.

When you have selected your casegoods, check on availability before placing your order. Delivery delays are a problem you'll encounter in buying all types of furniture, but casegoods delivery delays are the worst. Manufacturers hold orders until they have enough for an economical cutting; materials may be scarce; labor and production are slow; orders are again ganged for shipping. All in all, it's a long process. If you're in a hurry for your casegoods items, go to a store that has them in a warehouse.

KIDS' STUFF

Buying juvenile furniture involves a number of unique considerations, the most important of which is safety. The Consumer Product Safety

Commission estimates that 150 to 200 children die each year and 50,000 others are seriously injured in crib accidents. In response to these grim statistics, the federal government put specific safety standards for cribs into effect on February 1, 1974. All cribs manufactured after that date must conform to these standards, including:

1. Crib slats must be no more than two and three-eighths inches apart. This is to guard against the child's slipping through the slats feet first and being caught by the head.

2. The top of the dropside panel must be at least 26 inches above the mattress when the panel is set at its lowest level. This precaution is designed to help keep the baby from falling out.

3. The lock on the droprail should not be easy for the baby to open.

4. The crib must be of a standard size. Making each crib conform to size standardization insures a snug-fitting mattress. Such a fit will prevent the child from getting wedged in between the bed frame and the mattress.

Other requirements are just the very things parents should have been checking for in purchasing a crib: no sharp or rough hardware, sturdy drop latches, smooth wood surfaces, no splinters or cracks.

These new safety features add from $5 to $15 to the cost of a crib, but will surely make bedtime a safer and, therefore, happier time for all concerned.

Although you may want your child's bedroom to be in good taste, it is not recommended that it taste good to the child. Children chew cribs, and virtually all manufacturers use only nontoxic paints and finishes—but it doesn't hurt to check on this point anyway. One major manufacturer of juvenile furniture hangs tags on each crib to promote the fact that the crib sides are constructed of one piece of nontoxic, splinter-free molded plastic for extra safety. However, a cynical but experienced salesman pointed out that most kids chew on the panel ends—which in this case are all wood—not on the sides. Those cribs with wood side slats most often now feature plastic top rails to discourage chewing and prevent subsequent wood splinters.

Avoid plastic ornaments—balls, flowers, etc.—on a crib. They are dust-catchers and, worse, may be chipped, cracked or broken off by the baby, leaving sharp, ragged edges and splinters. Manufacturers have joined the proponents of early learning experiences, and some cribs now feature educational innovations. One such is the addition of clear plastic end panels which offer the child a clear view of his world through all four sides of his bed. (However, one young mother complained, "I think this crib was designed by Windex. After every nap and every morning that end panel is a mass of fingerprints, smears, spit and I-don't-like-to-think-what.") Following the work of behavioral scientists such as B. F. Skinner, cribs with a distinctly futurist flair have also been developed. One such sleep-play environment is round with clear-plastic panel walls. These removable and interchangeable panels may be mere windows or may feature items for the child to touch, watch (a fish tank) or play with. As the child's interests develop, these stimuli may be added to or replaced. The floor raises and lowers, as does the dome-like roof which is faced with mirrored, colored and clear panels. The special merits of such cribs are psychological and educational, and they are not best appraised as furniture.

With or without educational features, most cribs are delivered on a do-it-yourself assembly basis. One retailer offers this tip: If the drop panels are properly assembled and still screech whenever raised or lowered, try rubbing the metal rails with wax paper.

The time factor

After safety you must consider the length of time an item of juvenile furniture will be used. The average child sleeps in what is misleadingly called a six-year crib until he is two to two and a half years old. Therefore, no matter how adorable the crib and how precious your child would look in it, it is folly to spend hundreds of dollars for it.

Manufacturers routinely turn out canopied cribs, pastel cribs, cribs trimmed with fat pink rabbits, but the loving mother is offered the enticement of much more novel creations. For example, the heir might be tucked into a stagecoach replete with shotguns, window shades, strongbox and shoddy construction. Also harking back to the Old West is a covered wagon that offers less realistic detail than the stagecoach . . . but presents mother with more of a challenge in changing the bedding. A sleek red Fiberglas racing car strikes a more modern note—but retailers report that striking the Fiberglas (as kids are bound to do) produces serious cracks. These beds cost hundreds of dollars each and are so big that most kids' bedrooms would be crowded—if not crammed—by them. They provide total environments not only by design but by sheer size.

Children grow and change rapidly, and the covered wagon that is such fun at five may well be an embarrassment to a 12-year-old. So, although such "imaginative" beds may be fun to indulge in, you cannot expect to get much service from them unless you plan a large family, with child after child taking his turn in the stagecoach.

This same principle applies to the other furniture to be purchased for a child's room. Use wallpaper, bedspreads, pillows, posters and curtains to create a child's fantasy, if you wish; all of these can be chucked after a few years' use without guilt or serious budget problems. Dressers, chests, seating pieces and carpets are not so readily disposable, however.

A six-foot-long velvet shoe—à la old-woman-who-lived in-a-shoe—is eye-catching, will probably delight your child, will cost a couple of hundred dollars and will soon be outgrown. Dressers and chests decorated with clowns, chubby animals or daisies are, again, a poor investment because of the time factor. Far better to purchase casegoods that will blend first with the crib and, later, equally well with more grown-up furniture. Colorful campaign furniture is a big favorite because it works well for the very young child and for the teen-ager.

The older child and the teen-ager have furniture designed especially for them, too, of course. Stack units and room groups featuring an endless combination of chests, bookcases, desks and cabinets are flexible, provide space for youngsters' collections and hobbies. In fact, some of the best ideas for space-saving bedroom furniture for all ages can be found in kids' furniture. Stanley Furniture found that one of its youth groups—which was definitely styled for kids, as it featured a duck motif on drawer and door fronts—was being bought by adults for themselves. The adults appreciated the style and functionalism enough to make the effort to remove the ducks.

In addition to the ever-popular bunk and trundle beds, manufacturers are turning out storage beds that appeal to singles and studio-apartment dwellers, as well as kids. Storage beds have drawers built in under the bed. A bunk bed may have an attached bookcase-desk in place of a footboard, and some storage beds feature add-on drawers for headboards and/or footboards. One firm seems to have reached the ultimate in space-saving bedding as it combines a bed, wardrobe, mirror, desk, bookcase-hutch, dresser, ladder and bulletin board in one unit.

Teen-girls' furniture is usually offered in an assortment of feminine colors, while teen-boys' furnishings generally come in maple or oak for the rugged all-man look. Again, apart from the space-savers that might appeal to any age group, there is no economy in buying "teen furniture." Teens are a very few years from being adults with mature tastes and preferences.

When purchasing juvenile casegoods, apply the same standards you would to a bedroom set for yourself. Be especially interested in marproof tops to guard against the inevitable bangs and scratches. Sturdy hardware is another must if the piece is expected to give years of service. Remember, too, when considering scaled-down children's furniture, that you will spend years bending down to those drawers as you care for your child's clothing—another good reason to buy standard-sized furniture.

KD—DO-IT-YOURSELF FURNITURE

KD (knockdown) furniture is often labeled "fun furniture" in ads—but anyone who ever spent Christmas Eve struggling to put together EZ Quik Assembly toys knows it's no fun. For years traditional retailers turned their backs on KD furniture, claiming, "It isn't furniture at all." Well, maybe KD isn't "furniture," but since they changed the name to ETA (easy-to-assemble) or, even better, "modular furniture," more and more home furnishings retailers of all types—department stores, chains, discounts and traditional stores—are carrying it. Of course, some home furnishings dealers always did carry KD—only they didn't say so. These dealers had it shipped in, assembled it themselves and featured it with traditionally-crafted furniture.

In the past KD was found in the housewares departments and, in fact, still is in many stores. Where-to-put-it seems to be a major hang-up with retailers who like KD but can't classify it. No matter where they put it, KD has some strong pluses from the retailers' point of view. It eliminates warehousing, inspection and storage problems; shipping costs are low; and it offers a quick turnover rate for a relatively small area of floor space.

Speed, cost and mobility are the big advantages KD offers the consumer. An entire living room set can be taken home in the trunk of a car and assembled immediately—no long wait for delivery. Although Macy's has tagged KD "The Affordables" and the cost is a fraction of that of traditionally-crafted furniture, it sells right across the economic lines.

When it's time to move on, KD is ready to go on the spur of the moment. Just disassemble and pack in a box.

Parsons tables, bookcases, record cabinets, wall units and desks have been KD standbys for years. Now such diverse items as stereo consoles, gun cabinets, sofas, love seats, bars, and rocking chairs are joining the low-priced KD ranks. KD is big in second homes, rec. rooms, dens, and singles' apartments.

KD furniture, of course, simply cannot be judged by the standards ordinarily applied to traditionally-produced furniture. Most KD furniture is of manmade—sometimes recycled—materials, such as plastics, laminates, compressed fibers, steel and aluminum.

The construction depends to a large extent on you and your skill at following directions. You will not need fancy tools to assemble your KD purchase; a screwdriver should do, and if you fasten bolt *A* to nut *B* in hole *C* properly, your KD purchase should perform adequately.

There are some KD construction features you can check. For example, all exposed surfaces should be finished. When the furniture is assembled, there should be no sharp edges exposed. You cannot expect drawers to be dovetailed, with center guides and dust panels, but the drawers should fit their openings squarely and move in and out without binding or tipping. The color or finish should be uniform throughout, and certainly all components should match perfectly. Defective parts, misfits and missing components are the natural hazards of KD, so unpack and check your purchase as soon as you get it home.

This instant furniture is inexpensive, eliminates delivery hang-ups and is easily portable. It can be slick, colorful and fun or just plain utilitarian. But no matter how you put it together, it isn't honest-to-God furniture to have and to hold, to love and to cherish, to pass on from generation to generation or even to admire with pride of ownership.

UPHOLSTERED FURNITURE—INSIDE AND OUT

Upholstered goods constitute, almost without exception, the most important category for the full-service retail home furnishings store. In 1972 the value of manufacturers' shipments of upholstered furniture topped the $2 billion mark—up 66 per cent in five years, according to the U.S. Census Bureau. A lot of upholstered furniture is being bought every day—and usually with little more thought than a consideration of the color of the fabric.

Of course, the fabric is the first thing you notice about a piece of upholstered furniture. A badly-chosen upholstery fabric can ruin an otherwise well-designed chair and, conversely, an eye-catching fabric can disguise a multitude of sins in a poorly-constructed chair. The fabric is usually the single most expensive ingredient in upholstered furniture and, according to DuPont, can account for 25 per cent or more of the total manufacturing cost. Unfortunately, it is also the biggest complaint producer. Most often consumers complain of poor abrasion resistance, fraying and tearing. There are no minimum quality standards established by either the industry or the government.

Upholstery fabrics are graded by the manufacturer to indicate price levels. The grade indicates quality level—but quality may not mean durability, cleanability or strength. Some very expensive fabrics are also very fragile and are meant to be used only for decorative purposes—not for hard-wear use. The quality of upholstery fabric is determined by such things as the type of fiber used; the type of weave; special finishes (stain- and soil-resistant); whether the fabric is imported or domestic; the design. If, for example, the design is hand-screened or a limited-edition decorator pattern, it will cost more.

While industry spokesmen often recommend buying "the best upholstery fabric you can afford," this does *not* mean that *the most expensive* will be *the best* for you. A good, sturdy, hard-wearing, soil-resistant synthetic may be best for your purpose—although it will cost far less than a decorator silk.

Different suppliers use different grading codes. This is important to remember when comparison shopping. Manufacturer A's grading system does not equal the grading system of Manufacturer B. Each manufacturer uses his own system—making accurate comparison difficult, if not impossible. Despite the difference in codes, the system is the same: the fabric plus the cost of the basic piece in a muslin cover determines the price. Therefore, if the basic price of a sofa in a muslin cover is $500 and you choose a good-quality cover, you may increase the total cost by $100.

If the floor model is shown in a beige damask, for example, and you want the same fabric in green, the cost should not increase. You will, though, probably have to wait for your special color to be made up at the factory and delivered.

Another alternative is to supply your own fabric. If you wish to use the same fabric for your sofa that you have used for draperies, some manufacturers will permit you to do so. In this case, you will pay the cost of the sofa in the basic muslin cover plus a service charge plus the cost of your own fabric.

Low-priced upholstered furniture is not offered in optional fabrics nor can you use your own fabric. You must get into the medium-price range before you are permitted any options.

Selecting the right fabric

Confronted with swatch books filled with hundreds of cottons, synthetics, velvets, tweeds, damasks, and vinyls in every color known to man, how do you choose the right one for your home? First, you should establish the color you want and the price you can pay. Do so before you leave home. Don't try to choose on the basis that "When something hits me I'll know if it's right." Most colors are available at all price levels, and establishing your price limits will eliminate a certain number of fabrics immediately.

At most warehouse-showrooms or discount operations, the problem of dealing with swatch books does not arise. You purchase the seating piece just as it is shown on the sales floor. If you want another color or pattern, you will probably have to choose another piece of furniture.

Durability

If the piece of furniture to be upholstered is going to serve a purely decorative purpose—such as a petite boudoir chair does—you can select a delicate pink velvet. The same fabric would be a disaster in the family room. Also, you can probably get by with an inexpensive fabric on a piece that will get little use.

Arm caps (removable covers) will prevent the arms of your furniture from turning into soiled, frayed embarrassments. The caps may be an extra-cost item, but they're worth the few dollars' investment. Some manufacturers that do not offer arm caps will make extra material available so that you can make your own. Ask about it.

Soil-resistant finishes have made it possible to select lighter shades for hard-wear use—but don't get carried away. No matter what kind of wonder finish a fabric features, it will still soil, and you'll still have to clean it.

Fibers and weaves

You will probably choose your upholstery fabric on the basis of touch and appearance—most shoppers do—but it will help to know a few basic facts about fiber and weaves. As a general rule, the tighter the weave, the stronger the fabric. Don't rely on a glance at the fabric surface to determine the tightness of the weave. Take a swatch of the fabric and hold it up to the light. You should not see light between the threads.

Check the fabric back. A light latex or acrylic coating on the back of less tightly woven fabrics adds extra strength and wear. The key word here is "light"; backing that is too heavy may be a sign of poor-quality fabric.

There are two basic kinds of upholstery fabrics—flat and pile. Flat fabrics have relatively smooth surfaces, although variations in weaving and yarns used can create special surface effects. The three basic types of flat fabrics are plain, jacquard and novelty.

Flat fabrics

Plain: This is the simplest weave of all and is done by interworking two yarns—over and under, just like darning. Satin, twill, denim and homespun are typical of the plain fabrics.

Jacquard: The pattern is woven right into the fabric through the use of a special loom. Jacquards may be woven from any of the major fibers and include brocades, brocatelles, damasks, and matelasses. Tapestries are also jacquard fabrics that are woven in more than one color.

Novelty: Novelty fabrics use broken weave patterns or yarns that are deliberately irregular in color or size. Tweeds with their "knots" and bumps, slubbed shantung and nubby bouclé are all common novelty fabrics.

Pile fabrics

Frieze: An upholstery fabric that has been around for a long time, rising and falling in popularity, it's really hard-wearing, with surface loops of nylon or wool on a backing generally of cotton or rayon. Check the loops on this one. They should be dense, well-packed and close to the surface. Loose slubs tend to break off.

Velvet: All the surface loops in a velvet weave are cut to form a short pile. Silk velvet is more expensive—but not longer-wearing—than cotton velvet, and there are many grades of both. Cut velvet, crushed velvet, pressed velvet and velour (a short, dense velvet) have been used extensively in Mediterranean and Spanish styles in recent years. Synthetic fibers and soil-resistant finishes have made what was once a very fragile fabric more suitable for daily use.

Plush: This is an overgrown velvet. The pile simply hasn't been cut as short as velvet pile.

Vinyls   Vinyls, of course, are not woven at all but are chemically created. Vinyl chloride—which presents health problems in its manufacture, but not as finished product—is applied to a backing to create a leather-like or "wet-look" surface. Naugahyde, Boltaflex and Koroseal are well-known vinyl brand names. Vinyls come in graded weights and may be supported or unsupported. (Supported vinyl has a fabric backing that makes it stronger.) Vinyl is easy to clean and is often used on furniture designed for hard use. Unless specially fabricated, vinyl often feels clammy, particularly in humid weather. You will notice that much vinyl-covered furniture is tufted. This is because the tufting creates air pockets between the vinyl and the person sitting on it, thereby lessening the clammy feeling.

Technical innovations will continue to produce new upholstery fabrics and fibers. Knitted textiles do not now play a significant role in the upholstery industry, but with technical improvements that situation is expected to change.

Natural fibers   The natural fibers—cotton, wool, linen and silk—are well known to most of us. As you might expect, silk is the most delicate. Cotton takes color very well and blends easily with other fibers. Good-looking linen tends to wear quickly unless teamed with other fibers. Quilting will add to the durability, life, luxury and cost of both cotton and linen. The thing to watch for in buying a quilted fabric is the stitch. A chain stitch will pull out if one stitch is broken. A lock stitch will hold firm.

Moths and mildew take their toll on natural fibers—as do stains, unless the fabric has been given the benefit of one of the soil-resistant treatments such as Scotchgard or Zepel. These finishes are certainly a big help in keeping your furnishings stain-free, but they are all too often oversold. They *protect* the fabric but *do not make it impervious* to any and all stains. They certainly cannot make a poor-quality, loosely-woven fabric stronger or more durable.

The only sure way to tell if a fabric has been treated with a stain-resistant finish is to look for a label. You can't see or feel such a finish.

Natural fibers are easy to identify by name, but synthetics are usually marketed under the manufacturer's brand name. For example, Herculon is not a fiber, but is a brand name for an olefin fiber; Kodel is a brand name for a polyester. Remember to evaluate upholstery fabrics by the fiber, not the brand name.

Manmade fibers   (Of the manmade fibers listed below, only rayon is susceptible to mildew—an important consideration if you live in a humid region.)

Acetate: This is not a strong fabric for upholstery use. It doesn't resist abrasion and also tends to wrinkle. Celanese and Estron are two well-known acetate brand names.

Acrylic: Acrylic cleans easily and wears moderately well as upholstery fabric. However, it pills and has poor resistance to abrasion. The "fun furs" are acrylic constructions. Acrylic brands are Acrilan and Creslan.

Nylon: Nylon has a lot going for it as an upholstery fabric. It is exceptionally strong and durable, abrasion resistant, wears well, cleans easily and takes color well. In fact, it is often used in combination with less durable fibers to add toughness. On the minus side, nylon stretches, pills and soils as easily as it cleans. Antron and Enkatron are two nylon brand names.

Olefin: Another toughie, olefin is a bulky, "tweedy" fiber that resists abrasion, is highly stain-resistant, and cleans easily. It is, however, highly sensitive to heat. Herculon is a well-advertised olefin.

Polyester: The polyesters—like Dacron and Fortrel—are durable, but because they make into very thin fabrics, they are seldom found as upholstery covers.

Rayon: These fabrics tend to lack dimensional stability; that is, they lose shape and bag and droop. Rayon wrinkles easily and has a low resistance to both abrasion and mildew. Used in combination with another fiber, such as nylon, rayon turns in a good performance. Marketed under such brand names as Tusson and Zantrel, rayon is a soft, comfortable fabric that takes dyes well and is offered in a wide range of glowing shades.

The style of furniture you select will determine to some extent what fiber and weave you use. That is, you aren't going to find a sturdy olefin fabric on a French Regency chair or a cut velvet on Early American. In general, traditional furniture styles are found in velvets, jacquards, and flat weaves, such as satin. Provincial styles use textured weaves and tapestries, and the rustic Early American designs are often found in homespun, cotton-blend prints and tweeds. Modern furniture often is offered in "natural"-looking fabrics—nubby wools, homespun, tweeds and textures.

Tailoring

When you buy clothing you check the tailoring as well as the fabric. Well, check the tailoring on your furniture too. The seams or welts should be straight and precise. Pull gently at a seam to check the tightness of the stitches. Bias-cut welts are strongest, and narrow welts are neatest.

If you choose a patterned fabric, make sure the pattern is matched. Stripes and plaids should run straight and true and should line up—cushions, backs, sides—right down to the floor. If the fabric has a center motif, such as a cluster of flowers, it should be centered on *each* cushion. If the floor sample is shown in a solid color and you are specially ordering a print, have the retailer's *written* assurance that the fabric will be properly matched.

Remove the seat cushions and check the "deck" on which they sit. It's best if the deck is covered in the same fabric as the rest of the piece, but it should at least be covered in a good-quality fabric that is color-co-ordinated or matched to the upholstery fabric. Now look at the back of the sofa or chair. It should certainly be covered in the same fabric found on the front and cushions, but sometimes low-priced furniture features a similar but lower-grade fabric on the back.

Tufting is an expensive feature of upholstered furniture. Salesmen tend to "confuse" tufting and buttoning in the enthusiasm of the sales pitch. In tufting, an area of fabric is folded, tacked down and stuffed individually for extra fullness and flexibility. Buttoning looks pretty much like tufting—only it costs less to do and should cost you less too. In buttoning, a button is placed on a flat upholstered surface and tacked to the inner filling. If the piece you are considering is buttoned, make sure the buttons are not just tacked on the fabric, but are securely tied down. Gently lift the button. You should be able to see the tie-string and feel the tension. It's really best just to avoid buttons on low-priced furniture. If not properly secured, the buttons can cause discomfort and will pull out, leaving a hole for filling to spill through.

The skirt should hang smoothly and evenly. In medium- and low-priced furniture the skirt is usually attached to the frame with a power staple gun. This isn't necessarily bad, but unless it is done carefully, the skirt will not hang evenly and smoothly. No matter how the skirt is applied, it should be free of wrinkles, gaps, sags and bunches.

Undercover work

All those old sayings like "Beauty is only skin deep" and "You can't tell a book by its cover" apply to upholstered furniture. For all you know, the gorgeous chair covered with super-de-luxe cut velvet could be stuffed with mouse hair and spiders' legs. It might all be resting on a frame of used toothpicks. You don't have any way at all of knowing what's in there by just looking.

The flashy chromium base of this glass-topped table flips on its side to create a cocktail table and can be up-ended to provide a dining table. Dual-function furnishings save space while stretching furnishing dollars. *(Selig)*

Even the smallest dining room can accommodate this traditional, never-out-of-style corner cabinet. It offers storage space as well as lighted shelves to display collectors' items.
(Thomasville Furniture Industries)

This velvet and vinyl shoe chaise is a temptation for any indulgent parent—a temptation to be resisted. Almost six feet long, it would fill the play area in most kids' rooms and the novelty is sure to wear out before the chaise does.
(Carson's of High Point)

This "Uni-Bed" is an example of the kind of functional design that can be found in kids' furniture. Carrying consolidation to the ultimate, this unit neatly combines a bed, chest wardrobe, desk, hutch, mirror and bulletin board.
(Schoolfield Furniture Industries)

The "Nu Dimension" collection of easy-to-assemble furniture has piled up awards for innovative design, ease of assembly and use of plastics. Each piece is delivered in a carry-out box the size of a suitcase. When you're ready to move on, so is the furniture. *(Decorian Division of Stratford)*

One mismatched stripe and the symmetry of the entire piece would be destroyed. (By the way, this trim sofa conceals a bed.)   *(Simmons)*

Split-back lounge chair has a molded urethane shell cushioned with foam and covered with a new suedelike vinyl. It's a technological accomplishment designed for hard wear that still looks and is comfortable.   *(Shelby-Williams)*

Button, button, who's got the button? This Queen Anne chair features diamond tufting on both seat and back. To ensure both wear and beauty, see that buttons are properly fastened. *(Ethan Allen)*

Using traditional furnishings in new ways can be both aesthetically and economically appealing. Here American primitive designs are worked in a sophisticated American synthetic to produce rugs designed for use on a bare floor or over wall-to-wall carpeting, or as wall-hangings. *(Concepts International)*

Indulge your fancy for fads in modestly priced accessories that can be replaced when the fun fades. These geometric Art Deco style lamps add instant freshness and zing to a room at minimum expense. *(Tyndale)*

Colored in vivid reds and yellows, this printed carpet not only zaps you with these relentlessly happy faces but offers gameboards, too. It's great fun for the first week, but how about the first five years? *(Jorges)*

In her book *How to Invest in Beautiful Things Without Being a Millionaire* (David McKay Co., Inc., 1971), Elaine Cannel writes that upholstered furniture is "the blindest item on the market. Without being able to see the wood, the construction, or even the material used for the stuffing, you usually have to go on faith in the store or manufacturer." Plus a few paltry guides along the way.

One of these guides is the manufacturer-applied label that is required by federal law to be attached to all upholstered furniture. This label must spell out the exact materials used as filling. The tag usually begins "Do Not Remove Under Penalty of Law." This time, instead of making jokes about being arrested for tearing off the tag, read it. The type of cushioning used will have a lot to do with the comfort, resilience and durability of the furniture. Also, the choice of cushioning material is sometimes a price-linked option. That is, you may be able to buy the same chair in a selection of cushion fillings. So learn something about the cushioning materials you are likely to meet on labels.

Down: You can't beat down for all-out luxurious comfort. You also can't beat down for cost. This is the most expensive cushioning material and, naturally, is found in only the most expensive furniture. Feathers-and-down is a wee bit less expensive than all-down. A drawback of both—besides cost—is that you have to keep plumping up the cushions because they mash down when you sit on them. And feathers can trigger allergy problems. Sometimes down is used in combination with springs; you lose some of the softness, but then you spend less time plumping up the cushions.

Latex Foam Rubber: Latex foam rubber provides a comfortable but firm seat that bounces back into shape when you get up. You may find furniture cushioned with a combination of foam rubber and down for extra surface softness. Density of the foam rubber core has a lot to do with how long the cushion will hold up. A good, dense foam rubber has many tiny air holes close together.

Polyurethane Foam: Polyurethane foam is one of the ubiquitous plastics that are making such deep inroads into furniture construction. It costs somewhat less than foam rubber, is a bit lighter in weight and "sits" equally well. It won't rot or mildew and is, in fact, extremely resistant to moisture. All of these qualities have teamed up to make polyurethane the most popular upholstery cushioning on the market. And when it is merged with a polyester fiber to produce polyurethane foam-fiber fill, you've got what many people think is the best cushioning around. In this blend the polyurethane foam is wrapped with a fluffy polyester fiber, such as Dacron, to produce a bouncy, fluffy cushion.

Of course, density plays an important role in the success of a polyurethane cushion. Slabs of low density foam can "sit out" quickly.

Polyester: Polyesters are usually used in tandem with a foam, but may also be used alone for a downlike softness. They are lightweight, odorless and nonallergenic.

Hair: Hair from horses, cattle and hogs produces a firm, resilient cushion. It is often rubberized for even more resilience, is fairly expensive, but will last a long time. A side chair cushioned with hair will probably remain resilient longer than you will. Allergies can be a problem with hair cushioning.

Cotton: Cotton is low on everybody's list of best-loved cushions. It lacks bounce, resilience and firmness and is susceptible to mildew and moisture.

Kapok and Sisal: These are plant products that are noteworthy mainly for low cost. They are subject to mold and mildew, can cause allergies, break down and crumble all too soon, and have almost no bounce.

How much of one of these cushion fillings has to be used before a piece of furniture falls into the "overstuffed" category? Any piece of furniture that is completely upholstered is called overstuffed. The term means that the stuffing has been put *over* the frame. The scantest, most thinly-padded chair may be called "overstuffed" if no wood is exposed.

Cushions come not only with a selection of stuffings, but in a variety of shapes and styles too. A *loose back and seat* refers to separate cushions that are upholstered on all sides, but are not attached to one another or to the back of the chair or sofa. *Tight back and seat* refers to sofas and chairs that do not have separate cushions. *Slip seats* are separate and can be lifted out of the frame. They are usually found on side chairs or pull-up chairs.

To prolong the life of the upholstery fabric, look for loose cushions that, on a sofa, are all of the same size and shape so that you can reverse and interchange them. *T*-shaped end-cushions on a sofa—with more than two cushions—limit rotation.

Of course, there is more to the construction of upholstered furniture than the cushions, but you're not going to be able to see it. You will have to rely on asking questions and on your own "sit before you buy" tests. Assuming you have chosen a reputable dealer who will stand behind his merchandise, ask your salesman: How is the frame constructed and what is it made of? The frame should be hardwood—not plywood or particle board—and should be kiln-dried to prevent warping. The joints should be double-doweled—not stapled—and glued, with corner blocks added for strength.

You cannot expect the wood used in the covered frame to be the same as that used for any exposed parts. Any exposed wood should be well-finished and should conform to the same standards you would apply to the wood used in casegoods.

Molded polypropylene frames are a recent innovation designed to reduce production costs. They are strong and lightweight but, like all-steel frames, have not been in use long enough for consumer reports to have been made.

What kind of springs are used? Two kinds of springs are used in upholstered furniture—coil and flat. Hand-tied springs give excellent service, but hand-tying is a slow process that drives up production costs. As a result, you will find hand-tied coil springs only in the most expensive furniture. Coil assemblies, machine-made as a unit, are found in most furniture and will give good service. Either kind of coil spring should be framed around the top edge with a heavy wire to hold the springs in place and give a firm, sag-resistant edge to the seat. If you press down on the edge of the seat, you should be able to feel this spring edge.

What kind of webbing is used to support the seat? Any webbing—steel, nylon or synthetic fabric—should be wide and closely interlaced to prevent springs from pushing through the bottom of the chair.

There have been experiments by some manufacturers using foam cushions for upholstered furniture without springs or frames. This, as might be expected, gives a rounded, smooth-lined appearance, but is too new to comment on regarding wear.

Now, with the answers to these questions in mind, apply your own performance tests. Feel the piece of furniture you are considering. Run your hands over the back and arms. If it's well padded, you shouldn't feel any bumps or hard edges.

Sit on it. Is it comfortable? Too soft? Too firm? Bounce up and down. The springs should help you bounce—and should not creak or make noises. When you bounce and wiggle, the frame should remain firm and stable. Now lean back hard. Does the frame still feel secure? You shouldn't feel the upper edge of the frame through the padding.

Get up and give the chair the knee as a test of the frame. Put your knee against the outside of one arm, reach across and pull the other arm toward you. Neither arm should yield.

Finally, have someone else—preferably someone fairly heavy—perform these same tests. While he is testing, you watch the chair for sags, droops and weaknesses. If you are considering a sofa, you and your co-testers should both sit on the sofa. The springs should be installed so that you don't roll together or bounce one another.

Where the action is

The industry term "action furniture" applies to recliners, rockers and sleep sofas. While most of the quality tests and problems that apply to standard upholstered goods may also be applied to action furniture, there are some special considerations to keep in mind when shopping for the latter.

Recliners

Even though recliners account for 25 per cent of total chair sales, surveys have indicated that 85 per cent of the people who like the idea of a recliner are turned off by the size and styling of most of them. Traditionally, recliners have been big, bulky items covered in sturdy but not very attractive fabrics. They have been promoted on Father's Day and Christmas as appropriate gifts for Dad, to hide away in the den or family room. No more.

In an attempt to grab that reluctant 85-per-cent chunk of the market, manufacturers have been upgrading styles like wild. Synthetics and special treatments have added to the style range of upholstery fabrics available. Technical innovations, such as pop-up headrests, lower silhouettes and backs that require only inches in which to recline, have added to the desired high-style look.

The basic difficulty in choosing a recliner is the same as the difficulty in choosing any other upholstered furniture. As the October 1972 issue of *Consumer Reports* explained, "You can inspect—indeed specify—the cover material and get some impression of how well it's put on. You can check for personal comfort. You can evaluate the esthetics of a piece on the showroom floor. But you can't tell what's really going on inside without destroying the piece. And a lot goes on inside reclining chairs."

The *Consumer Reports* staff did destroy 15 different recliners and, as a result, came up with the following conclusion: "From what we have learned, the purchaser of a reclining chair can't go very far wrong.

Overall, our test models were remarkably sturdy and reliable instruments of comfort. That reduces our buying advice to what may seem like an elementary three-part exercise:

"1. Go for comfort. . . . 2. Go for style. . . . 3. Everything else equal, go for the lowest price." The "everything else" includes upholstery fabric, frame, cushioning and guarantee. Do get a guarantee that spells out exactly what parts are covered, for how long and under what conditions.

Sleep sofas

If you need something to sleep on every night, don't buy a convertible sofa. It's fine for a guest room or occasional use, but for every night . . . better not. As a mattress-maker explained, "There is no way to make a mattress at the right price for use in a hide-a-bed that will provide comfort. A good-quality mattress is priced out of the sleep-sofa market." Also, you aren't going to enjoy folding and unfolding the sofa every morning and night, no matter how smoothly the mechanism operates.

Convertibles have in recent years become more comfortable as sofas, but as beds they run a poor second to sleeping on a bag of potatoes.

As you would when selecting a recliner, check a convertible's upholstery cover, frame, cushioning and mechanism. No matter how confined the display area, insist that you be permitted to open the sofa yourself. Don't let the salesperson help you. If it's too heavy in the store, it will be too heavy at home.

Comparison shopping—the near-impossible dream

You'll find comparison shopping for upholstered furniture a real struggle. There are so many variables—and so many of those variables are concealed—that for all practical purposes the task is virtually impossible. You would need a spec sheet listing manufacturer's name, model number, cover grade, frame construction, filling content, and spring construction. Tailoring and extra features, such as arm covers and casters, can also create price differences and belong on any checklist.

This does not mean, however, that you should not shop around for the best values. Look at the merchandise in several stores, get an idea of current prices, styles and guarantees. You will find that in order to purchase a chair of the quality you want, you must spend at least X dollars and no more than X dollars. Within that framework you can compare values.

The consumer protection movement is forcing manufacturers to establish standards and provide information on upholstered goods that may also affect your buying decisions. Flammability standards have been under discussion for some time; in early 1974, while the federal government was still at the discussion stage, California became the first state to require both the upholstery fabric and its fillings to pass stringent flammability tests. There is little doubt that federal antiflame standards will also be enacted—to the moans of manufacturers and the cheers of consumer action groups. The federal government is also expected to require manufacturers to provide consumer information tags giving data on the durability of the upholstery fabric used.

LAMPS AND ACCESSORIES

Lamps and accessories are known to the home furnishings industry as traffic-builders. That is, they bring in customers who are not really in the market for a major purchase—just a little something new to freshen up a room. Hopefully, then, the salesman can use his charm and persuasiveness to sell the shopper on a big-ticket item. It works more often than you might expect.

Display of lamps and accessories is often cluttered, but this is organized clutter deliberately contrived to excite the treasure hunter and keep the browser browsing.

When you are in the market for a lamp or accessory item, SHOP AROUND. This is one area where comparison shopping really pays off. Lamps are among the highest profit items for retailers, and many are priced to maximize that profit. If they don't move at the trial-balloon price, the merchant can cut the price for a big sale—down to the manufacturer's suggested retail price.

At a merchandising clinic for retailers in September 1974, consultant John A. Lennon advised merchants to mark up goods at more than double to protect their own profit pictures. Regarding lamps specifically, Lennon was quoted by *Home Furnishings Daily* as saying, "If I bought a lamp at $25 and it looked like a better lamp then I'd price it at $75." Such pricing may improve the dealer's financial picture, but it won't do much for yours.

Lamps are easy do-it-yourself delivery items, so you don't need to worry about shopping at a store with this service. Great new designs are quickly ripped off—to the dismay of designers—and turn up at all price levels. This means you can shop at all kinds of stores and find good-looking pieces. Try the warehouse-showrooms for super selection and visit some of the discounters for good buys. One big national discount chain usually features the current "look" in lamps at prices considerably under those of specialty and department stores.

Selecting lamps and accessories is not simply a price-comparison operation. They are vital to completing the personality of any room. In fact, simply with a switch in accessories, you can change the character of a room without the expense of refurnishing. This is the place to indulge your fondness for fads. If you wish, buy kooky lamps, zany-colored decorative pieces; then, when you tire of them, scrap them, with no great loss in dollars. You can dress up a $99 table with a good, well-designed lamp—or ruin the effect of a $300 table with cheap accessories.

Interior designers do about 20 per cent of their business in accessories and lamps—a reflection of the interest of consumers in this merchandise. Nathan Ancell, president of Ethan Allen, sees consumers as being increasingly aware of the sophistication and quality of lamps and accessories. He says, "With a $99 end table, the consumer may choose a $350 lamp, or with a $200 étagère, she may choose to accessorize the furniture with china and small accessories worth $2,000."

Decorating books are full of how-to tips on lamp size and placement. Read them. Salesmen often offer the general rule that every living room needs five lamps. Don't you believe it. The size of your room and your other furnishings determine how many lamps you need. There is also no hard and fast rule that you must have a pair of lamps flanking your sofa. Again, shop around. Look at room displays, magazines, decorating books. You will find lamps and accessories fun to shop for. Accessorizing is a great way to express your personality through mixing and matching, using pieces from your personal collections, craft items and family heirlooms.

SEVEN

Getting the Best Bedding

Choosing the *right* mattress is important for a variety of reasons, some more serious than others. One, if you sleep eight hours a night, you spend one-third of your life in bed; two, according to Dr. Alex Comfort in his best-selling book *The Joy of Sex*, (Crown Publishers, 1972) beds are "still the most important piece of domestic sexual equipment"; and, three, the choice of your bed is often seen as an indication of your personality.

Pierre Plouffe, president of Head Bed Company, one of New York's most fashionable custom bedding firms, believes your choice of mattress is linked to your personality and reports that "It's amazing how many people come in here trying to cover up the kind of person they really are, by starting out saying they want something very simple, and walking out having ordered a headboard trimmed in gold." Perhaps some of us buy mattresses for the persons we *wish* we were: Plouffe sells his seven-foot-diameter round beds to suburban matrons in their fifties.

You will probably buy your mattress at a department or furniture store—78 per cent of mattress-buyers do, according to a recent survey sponsored by Sealy. The same survey indicates that the bedding customer places a good deal of trust in brand names, store reputation and value. She is not so much concerned with features—how many coils, how thick, type of filling—as she is with what those features will do for her. To find out, she will rely on the advice of a salesperson.

Far better when you are spending money on bedding to do a little homework and rely on your own basic knowledge coupled with specific information from the salesperson. A good innerspring mattress will last for ten to fifteen years. During those years you will be glad you took the time to buy the right bedding.

If you begin your shopping for bedding by browsing through ads, you are likely to find a heavy stress on brand names and package deals. For years, retailers promoted what was called the 2+2+2 combination (two twin headboards, two mattresses, two box springs) to get the shoppers distracted from shopping for just a mattress. Today the four-piece outfit (mattress, foundation, headboard and frame) is most frequently advertised—still the package versus individual items. Real package-minded retailers offer six-piece packages—two pillows, two sheets, two pillowcases—free when you buy a mattress-foundation set. Concentrate on buying the mattress and foundation and don't be lured into buying a low-quality set just to get some bed linens that will be long worn out while you are still trying to sleep on a sagging mattress.

Shoppers tend to place confidence in the major brand names in bedding. All of the major manufacturers turn out good products, but they all make a full line of mattresses to sell at varying price levels. Their promotional or low-priced products can be real duds. You want to get the best mattress for yourself and your needs at the best possible price. Don't shop by brand alone.

Less reputable dealers may also use respected brand names simply to draw customers into the store and then switch them to inferior products which bring the store a bigger profit. In *The Great Discount Delusion,* (David McKay Co., Inc., 1965) by W. H. Nelson, John W. Hubbell, vice president of Simmons Company, producers of Beautyrest mattresses, explains this strategy: "A case in point is a large discount store in New York which advertised the fact that it had Beautyrest mattresses at cut prices, despite the fact that it was not an authorized sales outlet for the Simmons Company. Many customers told us our merchandise was maligned in this discount house. This was not a surprise, because the store found it necessary to degrade our merchandise to avoid selling it. (It was difficult for the store to get a supply on the one hand, and they had to sell it at a loss on the other hand.) One of our employees and his wife went to this discount house as shoppers and were exposed to a tirade of untruths about the Beautyrest mattress. This discount house advertised the Beautyrest because it wanted to attract trade. It felt that it would be able to cope with the situation by sales manipulation [polite word for misrepresentation]. The store switched consumers to an inferior product which it could buy at a cheaper wholesale price."

You don't use price as a single signpost of quality in any other home furnishings purchase. Don't do it with bedding either. You can't get top-quality bedding at bargain-basement prices, but some retailers charge all the traffic will bear on bedding. In their folder "Things to Know About Bedding" the now-defunct Home Furnishings Council says, "Because mattresses do not go out of style as quickly as do dresses, because they do not deteriorate in storage, and because they are not often purchased by the store in large quantities, there is very little need for price cutting or 'sale' merchandise. As a result, the price of bedding becomes a kind of 'bench mark' of the value of its materials, design and workmanship. The price charged for bedding often gives you a clue to its value." Hmmmm—that's the kind of consumer advice that can lead you directly to the poorhouse.

Despite the fact that industry surveys have shown that consumer income is relatively unimportant in the bedding purchased—that is, a low-income consumer is just about as likely to buy top-of-the-line bedding as is a high-income shopper—the bedding industry seems to try to defend both sides of the cost issue: "no cost is too great" and "good bedding costs almost nothing."

Salesmen are exhorted to "always talk pennies, never dollars" when selling bedding. In its consumer booklet *How to Buy a Mattress* Simmons says that a mattress selling at $79.50, based on a fifteen-year guarantee, costs about 1-1/2 cents a night—"much less than a sleeping pill or less than a whiff of perfume." Then it quickly switches sides again: "But these days, who puts a price tag on one's health and well-being?"

One thing is sure: you're not going to pay for that mattress at one and one-half cents a night. You're going to pay for it all in one hefty chunk . . . plus tax. Keep your eye on the bottom line and remember your budget.

HOW BIG IS BIG ENOUGH?

Before you actually go out mattress-shopping, decide what size mattress you want. Size is the one thing that is standard in shopping for bedding. One manufacturer's Firm may be another's Super Firm; one's Medium may be the other guy's Firm. But sizes are standard.

At one time adults had two choices in mattress sizes—twin and full. In the early sixties supersizes were introduced, and you can now take your choice from the following selection of sizes:

Twin—39 inches wide x 75 inches long
Long twin—39 x 80
Full (also known as Double)—54 x 75
Long Full—54 x 80
Queen—60 x 80
King—76 x 80
Long King—76 x 84
California King (a size sold only in the Western states)—72 x 84

(The Hollywood bed is a merchandising package, not a bed size. The package consists of a twin-sized headboard, metal bedframe and mattress and box spring—no footboard.)

If you've been looking at mattress ads, you know that it's the supersizes—king and queen—that are getting all the promotion. The National Association of Bedding Manufacturers launched a campaign in April 1972 to promote the sales of supersizes and firmly establish the queen-size as the new "standard" double bed. Ads tell you that the old full-size is just ridiculous for two adults—it gives each sleeper only 27 inches of width. You are reminded that Americans are getting bigger and bigger and need suitably larger beds. Full-sized mattresses are sneered at as "cramp-sized," "old-fashioned" and "baby-sized."

It's true. You do get only 27 inches per person in a full-sized bed and you might well be more comfortable and sleep better on a bigger bed, but it isn't only your welfare that prompts manufacturers and retailers to push supersizes. Supersize bedding is more profitable to sell. Although prices and figures change rapidly, queen-size bedding brings 55 per cent more profit to the retailer than does full-size; king-size draws 43 per cent more. Every time a salesman can switch a customer from a full-sized mattress to a supersize, he boosts volume by 25 per cent for a queen-size and a whopping 87 per cent for a king-size. When stores work to show a per-square-foot net profit by department, you can see how supersizes can beat the inflation spiral for the retailer.

Because supersizes add such zip to the balance sheet, the retailer also uses special merchandising techniques for them. For example, it is common—and recommended—practice among retailers to show only twin-sizes and supersizes in the bedding departments. The frowned-upon full-sizes are exiled to a lowly position outside the bedding department. Simmons offers retailers display setups that showcase only twin-sizes, and queen-sizes—"no old-fashioned double-sizes." The ad for these display materials quotes a retailer as "firmly believing" that this display "is the reason they have converted so many shoppers for old-fashioned double-size mattresses into immediate buyers of the more profitable queen-size Beautyrest sets."

Don't misunderstand—this is not a dishonest sales technique. You will find that many reputable dealers use it. It is mentioned here to make you aware of the fact that you will be strongly urged, pushed, coaxed, cajoled and advised to buy supersize bedding. You may find yourself weighing the merits of a queen-sized mattress without realizing that it is queen-size—not the full-size you want. That's why it is so important for you to decide what size is best for you before you get to the store. Once you decide, stick to it. If you are strongly swayed by the salesman, go home and think it over. Maybe he's right—but then again, maybe he isn't.

When you are deciding on size, there are a number of factors to consider: first, size of the sleepers versus size of the mattress. Supersize ballyhoo notwithstanding, twin-size is still acknowledged as the best size for an individual sleeper. Its 39 inches give the sleeper more width than any other size, and, for those over five feet, eight inches tall, the long twin gives added length. Twins are easiest to make and turn, and allow each member of a couple to choose the preferred firmness.

When selecting mattress length, add ten inches to the height of the tallest person who will use the bed. That allows five inches of space above the head and five below for tucking in blankets and sheets.

Of course, you may not need a supersize mattress to accommodate your physical size; you may want it just because you like the idea of it. A great big bed can add *Playboy*-style glamour to even the most prosaic room. Perhaps a king-sized mattress best suits your lifestyle or personality or dreams. The Shah of Iran has a custom-made super-supersized bed—eight feet long and eight feet wide—to complement his regal ways.

No matter how regal your personality, though, you have to buy a mattress that you can fit into your bedroom. So keep in mind the size of the mattress versus the size of the bedroom. If you get a supersize, will you have room for any other furniture in the bedroom? Will you be able to open drawers and closet doors? Will you have room to walk around?

Can you get the mattress and foundation into the room? Sharp turns, narrow halls and low ceilings all make it extremely tricky, if not impossible, to maneuver supersizes. Keep this in mind, particularly if you plan to deliver your own bedding.

Room size is a big barrier to supersized sales, and salesmen are trained to attempt to overcome your objections that your room is just too small for a king- or queen-sized mattress. If your facts tell you that your room is too small, then don't be swayed; you're the one who will have bruises and banged shins from squeezing between the bed and dresser if you get a too-big mattress in a too-small room.

You don't have to worry about accommodating a queen-sized mattress on your full-sized headboard. Stretcher rails are made to convert the old headboard to take the new size. Some retailers run special deals in which they throw in the stretcher rails free when you buy a queen-sized set.

Don't forget to consider the cost of sheets and blankets for a super-sized bed. Larger pillows, too, will probably be needed. Supersized bed linens are superpriced and should be added to the total cost of the king- or queen-sized bed.

TICKING TO TURN YOU ON

You can't judge a mattress by its cover. One manufacturer instructs, "Don't buy a mattress for its good looks, but rather for your good looks after a good night's sleep." Good advice—but this same manufacturer came out with a line of tickings (the fabric mattress covering) designed by Oscar de la Renta that was promoted for its fashion flair. Some retailers stage fashion shows featuring mattresses and dresses in the same fabrics; others use snazzy tickings as wall coverings and draperies in store displays. Simmons even provides monogrammed mattresses for newlyweds. The salesman may tell you, "It's comforting to know that you are resting on a beautiful fabric instead of some drab old blue and white stripe." Ticking adds glamour to an otherwise strictly utilitarian product.

On the sales floor eye-catching ticking will capture the attention of the shopper. As one manufacturer explains it, "All the dealer sells is the way the product looks, feels and is priced. A woman's first reaction is to appearance, and a good-looking cover will get her immediate reaction."

Don't be sold on a mattress by its fancy cover. You'll just cover it with sheets and blankets anyway. In fact, you may be able to get a good buy if you watch for sales of mismatched bedding—foundation and mattress in different covers. The cover should be sturdy and close-woven; eight-ounce weight is preferred. Your concerns should be with quality, construction, comfort and cost, with aesthetic factors at the bottom of the list.

THE INSIDE STORY

Mattresses present many of the same problems you confront when buying upholstered furniture. There's a lot of concealed information in a mattress, and it's what's inside that will make the difference between years of sleeping comfort and sleepless misery.

Price is not the most important factor to mattress-shoppers. Comfort is. About 20 per cent of all bedding customers have backache problems. As Americans have become ever more health-oriented, mattress-makers have steadily increased their stress on the health aspects of their products. Sealy advertises, "No morning backache from sleeping on a too-soft mattress"; Simmons launched "The Hard Line" with an Orthopedic display; Spring Air has a "Back Supporter" mattress; Serta offers the "Ther-a-pedic."

Despite all the fancy medical-sounding names, Dr. Lawrence W. Friedman contends in his book (with L. Galton) *Freedom From Backaches* (Simon and Schuster, 1973) that "The best type of bed is a rigid surface covered by a simple horsehair mattress. It is not easy to buy; salespeople are often reluctant to sell such a mattress because it is the cheapest type available; they much prefer to offer an expensive orthopedic mattress which, coupled with boards, springs and other intricacies, ends up approximating the effect of the simplest, inexpensive horsehair mattress." If you are one of the six million Americans with backaches, this advice may well be worth thinking about.

There are two major classes of mattresses—innerspring and foam—and you can get a good night's rest on either. Before you decide which is best for you, there are a few construction facts to be aware of:

Innersprings

Innersprings have been around for a long time and are the more popular of the two mattress types. An innerspring mattress is made by enclosing steel springs or coils between layers of padded upholstery. There are two basic kinds of coils used—open and cloth-pocketed. The open coils are held together—and apart—by steel wires on a steel frame. A border wire around the edges gives extra support.

Cloth-pocketed coils are just what the name implies—coils enclosed individually in cloth pockets. The pockets are tied or sewn together.

Although ads often proclaim the number of coils used in a mattress as though it were terrifically important, the number of coils indicates little about the quality of the mattress. There may be as few as 180 or as many as 1,000 coils in a mattress. (Of course, a certain minimum is needed. Manufacturers often recommend that you have at least 200 to 300 coils— and at least 800 in cloth-pocketed coil-mattresses.) Holland Wire Products, Incorporated, a manufacturer of innerspring units, says, "High coil counts are an advertising gimmick—not a contribution to comfort or value. . . . For comparison, your auto engine does a fine job with six or eight cylinders. It could be built with ten or 12 or 20, but they aren't needed, so adding more than enough would just cause trouble."

More important than the number of coils in a mattress are the gauge and temper of steel used to make the coils and the design of the coils. Latex coating on the coils will help keep them noiseless; baked-on enamel will prevent rusting.

A layer of insulation goes over the coils to give buoyance to the cushioning materials—and to keep the cushioning out of them. The insulator may be made of wire, plastic, cotton net, hog hair, sisal or cotton. Next comes the cushioning which may be cotton, latex or urethane foam, hair, latex flakes (which may sift or pile up), wool or polyester.

All these materials must be fastened together to avoid bunching and shifting. Tufting used to be a popular method of doing this fastening, but for a variety of reasons—most recently the problem of flammability— tufting has slipped into oblivion. Almost all mattresses made today are made without tufting.

A cloth flange runs around the outer edge of the mattress panel. After the cushioning materials are in place, the flange is drawn over the border edge and anchored to the coils to keep the materials firmly in place. These edges should be tightly sewn and reinforced to withstand stress.

A quilted mattress is made the same way as the smooth-top, only before assembly the covering is prequilted to some or all of the cushioning and insulating materials.

When shopping, look for ventilation holes or ports. These ports will allow air to circulate to the inner materials. Check to be sure the ports are real—not just imitation.

Foam mattresses

Foam mattresses can be either latex (rubber) or urethane (plastic), or a blend of the two. They are nonallergenic, mildew- and mold-proof, need not be turned, and are light and flexible. The light and flexible part is important when you're moving. Foam is about half the weight of innersprings, and that flexibility will get you around corners with ease.

Both latex and urethane foam mattresses are available in various thicknesses. Although some manufacturers insist that you need at least six inches for comfort, four-inch thickness is fine—not even the princess of "Princess and the Pea" fame could quibble about those extra two inches. The four-inch mattress does, however, require a higher foundation to bring the top surface of the mattress to standard bed height. Do buy at least a four-inch-thick mattress; much less amounts to a pad, not a mattress. A Chicago-area warehouse-showroom advertised loud and long a full-sized foam mattress for an unbelievably low price. When shoppers went to the store to see the mattress, the salesmen tried to divert them to bedding at regular prices. When the shoppers insisted, they were shown a foam mattress measuring 54 x 75 . . . but only one and one-half inches thick. The old bait-and-switch game again.

Latex foam: Latex mattresses are molded with small hollow-core spaces—plus natural pores or air cells in the mattress. Large, loose core holes lead to sagging and buckling in no time. There is wide variety in the quality of latex foam, so ask to see a sample of the kind used in the mattress you are considering.

Urethane foam: Instead of being molded like latex, urethane foam is cut from large blocks of foam. High density is important in a urethane mattress, and there are those who believe urethane to be less resilient and firm than latex. In either latex or urethane go to extra-firm with a one-piece core (as opposed to thin layers sandwiched together) if you need good support.

Both latex and urethane foam need only ticking to complete the mattress construction. Although some makers may quilt the ticking directly to a thin layer of foam to envelop the core, there are no layers of insulation and cushioning needed as there are in an innerspring mattress.

THE FEDS MOVE IN

Despite industry screaming and hollering, in mid-1973 the federal government ruled that mattresses—not foundations—had to pass flammability standards set by the Department of Commerce. The bedding people estimate that it cost them $2.5 million to set up the standards for flammability—and no end of anguish and suffering just to save "some idiot" (one manufacturer's term for a burned-up consumer) whose mattress catches on fire.

There is doubt about how much protection the mattress flammability standards provide. The testing provisions relate to burning cigarettes on the surface of a bare mattress. The mattress must be fire-retardant: the cigarette will smolder, but not burst into flame. Of course, if you are smoking in bed, the bed probably has sheets and blankets on it. If they are in flames, you are not going to be appreciably better off because your mattress is only smoldering.

Your mattress should be clearly labeled that it does or does not (if left over from pretest days) pass the flame test.

IT ALL RESTS ON A FIRM FOUNDATION

Mattresses and foundations are promoted as sets. Over and over you will hear, "If you need a new mattress, you need a new foundation." *American Home's* book *How to Buy: Home Furnishings Guide* (Curtis Publishing Co., 1968) flatly says, "A box spring and mattress wear out simultaneously, and so they should be replaced simultaneously." It ain't necessarily so. One manufacturer says, "My box-spring unit should last 30 years with no trouble . . . but the mattress probably won't go beyond 15. I tell customers to check their box springs. Lie down on them and see if you can feel the springs poking up or sagging down. Roll around. Do you feel low spots? Do you roll to the center? Does one side sag more than the other? If so, you need a new foundation. Otherwise, your present one is probably in good shape."

Definitely do not buy a new mattress and put it on an old, *worn-out* foundation. Where the foundation sags, your new mattress will too. If you need both but can't afford both at once, wait until you can. You will save money in terms of wear and comfort.

The term box spring was often used interchangeably with foundation, but this is no longer accurate. There are now other foundations than box springs. The traditional coil-type box spring comes with fewer but heavier coils than does an innerspring mattress. Originally box-spring coils, like mattress coils, were hand-tied to hold them in position. Labor costs have made this process too expensive for mass production, so prebuilt units with wires, metal strips or small springs are now used. The coils sit in a wood frame on wood slats. The frame should be firmly joined of good, dry wood—but you don't stand much chance of ever seeing it to know if it is or not.

A layer of padding or filling material goes on over the coils to protect the mattress that will rest on them. Ticking, covering the top and sides, goes on over that. A thin cloth is stretched across the bottom simply to act as a dust shield.

You can get essentially the same coil springs without padding or covering too, but you're going to have to hunt for them. They are not standard items in many retail bedding outlets. Plain coil springs are less expensive than box springs, but you'll have to clean them more often. You may wish to add a layer of protective covering—a blanket or pad—over the springs to prevent rub-wear on the mattress cover.

Torsion-bar foundations use no springs at all, but are scientifically-designed steel bars that follow and second the support of the mattress. In this case, the mattress and foundation work as a system and should be bought as a pair.

Flat springs are the cheapest of all . . . and with good reason. They sag more quickly than any other foundation and have less bounce. Flat springs are just flat strips or links of steel that run horizontally across the frame.

A good foundation is important with any kind of mattress, but many experts say that it is even more so with a foam mattress. In this case, the foundation will absorb the stress while the foam gives comfort.

As a note of interest: the king-sized mattress requires two foundations—side by side—and these are sold only in pairs.

FRAMING IT

The frame supports both your foundation and mattress. Sometimes you'll find it included when you buy your bedroom furniture (too often it's the fifth item in "all five beautiful pieces for $399" instead of the nightstand), or the retailer may include the frame in the price of your bedding as a package deal. If you buy a Hollywood bed, the frame is always included.

Of course, a free frame is not a bargain if it won't do the job. You're paying for it in the total price anyway, so give it a careful once-over. Choosing a frame is not a big deal; just make sure it's strong enough to support your bedding. Sturdy, riveted legs are a must. Super-sized bedding should have a frame with a center bar running from foot to head for extra, much-needed support. The best bedding outfit will sag without adequate support from the frame. One manufacturer stresses that you should buy a frame with at least a one-inch-by-one-inch angle rail on the side bars to prevent the frame from bowing—and, consequently, the mattress from sagging.

U.S. Steel has developed a new box-spring design of steel with the legs bolted directly to the box-spring frame—eliminating the need for a separate bedframe. At this time the new frame is under consideration by bedding manufacturers, but has not yet gone into major production.

Casters may be an extra, but they are a nice feature on any bed as they make it easier to move for cleaning. They are particularly welcome on supersizes. Have two casters lock for stability and do get casters that are wide enough for the job and are suitable for your floor.

COMFORT

If you aren't comfortable on the mattress and foundation you buy, it doesn't matter how well-made, large or expensive they are. You can't tell if a mattress is going to be comfortable or not by just looking at it. You've got to try it out. So when you go shopping for a mattress, wear slacks. And don't go mattress-shopping feeling bone-tired; when you're exhausted, anything feels good. If two people will be using the mattress, they should both test it.

Lie down and stretch out. Is it long enough? Roll around—you should roll easily, without effort. Bounce up and down—the springs shouldn't make any noise.

Check for firmness, which is a matter of personal choice and has nothing to do with durability. Don't go for a too-firm or out-and-out hard mattress if it means sacrificing comfort. The mattress should have enough give to support all parts of your body—easing under your hips and shoulders, pushing up to support your lower back or side. Sit on the edge of the bed—it should be strong. You don't sleep on the very edge, but a strong border will help to keep the mattress neat and trim and prevent a hammock-like sag. When you get up, the mattress should bounce back to its original shape, and so should you.

When buying a box spring, lie down on it too. You shouldn't be able to feel the springs through the padding. Feel the underside of the box spring. There should be a horizontal wood slat supporting each row of coils or a metal frame providing the same support.

WATERBEDS

Although the interest in waterbeds has subsided to a mere trickle, the liquid beds are still with us. They are cheaper than more traditional bedding, but they will last only a fraction of the time; and many people feel that, even at their best, waterbeds will not be as comfortable. The amount of water you put in the bed determines how firm it becomes. Too much water and it's rocklike; too little and it's squishy. An unheated waterbed can be an actual health hazard. Early waterbeds had leakage problems, but manufacturers claim to have mopped these up in construction improvements and will happily exchange a sievelike bed for a watertight one. Small consolation when your bedroom is under water.

Manufacturers have made a few attempts to improve the waterbeds' image, with results that have been less than substantive. (For one thing, those in the business now call waterbeds "flotation beds.") But the beds were given an unexpected boost in early 1975, when a research group reported that waterbeds may be a boon to the bedridden by preventing or alleviating the severity of bedsores.

SHOP AROUND

Although, according to a Simmons survey, you will probably buy your bedding at the first store you shop at, this isn't a good idea. Visit several reputable dealers and try many makes and models before you buy. You and your mattress will spend a lot of time together over the years, and the time spent finding the right one will be amply repaid.

Apart from standard sizes, the bedding industry does not conform to any system of standards for firmness or quality. It has been reported that the Federal Trade Commission is exploring the possibility of establishing a grading system for mattress quality and performance, but until they do, you're on your own.

Each manufacturer sets up his own standards for Extra Firm, Firm, Medium Firm and so on; those standards do not relate to those of any other manufacturer. So you can't, for example, compare Sealy's Firm to Serta's Firm with any kind of accuracy.

There are some things you can do to compare. You can read the label. Bedding comes under FTC regulations that require a label showing the contents of the mattress and the amounts of material used. Make sure you are getting the contents the salesman said you were, and check to be sure all the materials used both inside and out are new.

The big bedding dealers have merchandise made specially for them by the manufacturers. They specify custom ticking or construction, and no other retailer gets the same merchandise. This means you can't shop for a specific mattress or foundation from one big store to another. However, you can still jot down the model number and brand name and shop at the little guys. (It's a good idea to make a note of the brand name and model number of the bedding you buy, too, so that you can check on delivery to make sure you get the items you purchased.) The little guys can't buy in large quantity and must take the standard items from the manufacturers' lines.

Chances are you can find a better deal on bedding prices if you shop at dealers in the outlying areas. Retailers in big-city, hot-competition areas generally hold to steady price lines to avoid self-defeating price wars.

Bedding delivery is not the problem that the delivery of casegoods is. You should have no problem getting prompt delivery. If you want your mattress and foundation set up, get a setup order in writing at the time you close the deal.

NEVER TO RETURN

Under state laws, once a mattress has been sold and delivered to your home, it is used. If you wish to return it, the retailer cannot resell it to another customer. Therefore, you're not going to find stores anxious to accept the return or exchange of a mattress. If, of course, it is damaged on delivery, the retailer should certainly replace it. Also, if you can show that your bedding is not properly constructed, the retailer can return it to the manufacturer. But if you just don't like it or find it uncomfortable, too bad. You're probably stuck with it.

John Wanamaker, the Philadelphia-based chain, gave bedding retailers fits in 1974 when the store ran a four-color mattress ad headlined "Take a Year to Try It Out." Other bedding retailers have made this offer, but Wanamaker's was done in such a big way by such a big firm that it attracted considerable attention from both consumers and retailers. In the past some bedding makers have backed up retailers with a 30-day trial on the top-of-the-line merchandise. But the one-year offer is something else—mostly a gamble on the store's part that most customers will keep their purchases.

EIGHT

Carpet-
the Big Putdown

"The carpet business is the worst there is. There are so many tricks you would be amazed." Those complaining words come not from a dissatisfied customer, but from a carpet retailer who is trying to operate honestly in the face of dishonest competition. Not only does he lose sales to the shady operator, but he suffers when people start to believe all carpet dealers are crooks. They definitely are not—but there are enough crooks around to justify consumer distrust. The Better Business Bureau, the Federal Trade Commission and the attorney general's offices have stacks of complaints on carpet purchases. The Special Assistant to the President for Consumer Affairs receives hundreds of complaints on poor-quality carpet that fades, mats and wears out almost instantly. Improper installation is another common gripe.

Don't be misled. The picture is not all dark. Today consumers can buy carpet at prices averaging 37 per cent below 1950 levels (installation costs, of course, have soared beyond those of 1950), and today's floor covering is longer wearing, better made and better looking. This is not due to some sort of mad philanthropy on the part of the carpet industry, but rather to improved technology and productivity, as well as reduced fiber prices and an enormous increase in annual sales. In 1950 annual

118

retail sales for floor coverings were under one billion dollars. In 1974 annual retail sales reached about five billion dollars.

If the industry is doing so well, why are so many consumers doing so badly? Buying carpeting is confusing—and some of that confusion is deliberate. Showrooms are a bewildering maze of hundreds, often literally thousands, of carpet samples in a seemingly infinite array of colors, a wide choice of fibers, a selection of weaves and, not least, a broad price range. Not only must one carpet be chosen from this overwhelming offering, but decisions must also be made on padding and installation.

Certainly it's great to have so many options, but in order to cope with this abundance in an effective and economical way, you have to make some decisions in advance . . . and this is just what most shoppers fail to do.

Although few people are likely to walk into a carpet department and decide on the spur of the moment to recarpet their homes, all too many carpeting decisions are made on impulse—and subject to persuasive sales talks. If you are going to shop wisely, there are several key decisions to make before going to the store.

This is true of any home furnishings purchase, but carpeting, by virtue of its cost and unique qualities, deserves to be viewed independently. Consumer action groups have found carpeting to be a leading source of complaints. You can head off many of your own problems and complaints by doing some advance work. The Carpet and Rug Industry Consumer Action Panel, an independent organization set up to settle consumer complaints about carpeting, strongly recommends that consumers inform themselves about carpet fibers, construction and colors so as to select the carpets best suited to their needs.

WHAT TO DO FIRST

Many studies have proved that when buying carpeting most shoppers consider color first and, in fact, are encouraged to do so. Decorating books advise the carpet buyer to "Choose appearance first." Manufacturers, decorators and retailers urge choosing color first in the hope that the buyer will get hung up on some six-color, double-level shag with a high price tag. That's wrong.

Sensibly, as with any home furnishings purchase, literally the first thing to consider is cost. When making other major investments—and, remember, carpeting is a major purchase that should last from ten to fifteen years—you first determine your price level and then shop. You don't look at mansions on a bungalow budget; you don't agonize over a Mercedes color chart when you have to finance a Volkswagen. Why do it with carpeting?

How much can you afford to spend—*total*? One hundred dollars, $1,000, $5,000? What percentage of your total home furnishings budget are you willing to devote to floor coverings (See Chapter 2)? Are you planning to pay cash, charge it or finance the purchase over several months (See Chapter 9)? Don't wait until you're in the showroom to make these financial choices. Make them with pencil and paper, consulting checkbook balance, present debts and future budget needs. You may find that you can't afford to buy at all—or that you can carpet two rooms instead of one.

Now that you have set a price limit for yourself, what can you buy with that amount? Area rug, room-size rug or wall-to-wall carpet? To people in the floor coverings business there is a difference between a carpet and a rug, although most shoppers use the terms interchangeably. Strictly speaking, a carpet comes by the roll in widths ranging from 27 inches up to 18 feet. A few carpets come in even wider widths, but the most common sizes are 12 and 15 feet. Rugs are finished on all four sides and are purchased in specific sizes and shapes. Generally, rugs lie loose on the floor; carpeting is fastened down.

AREA RUGS

Area rugs come in a variety of shapes and range in size from 3 x 5 to 12 x 15 (dimensions in feet). Of course, if you have a 12 x 15 room and buy an area rug of that size, you have defeated the purpose of the rug. An area rug should define or highlight an area—a conversation center, a dining area.

In the past, furniture and carpet stores largely left the sale of area rugs to department stores, but now most stores that sell floor coverings are featuring these rugs. From the dealers' points of view they offer relatively low handling costs and high profits.

Singles and young couples favor area rugs for both their decorative properties and their pick-up-and-go ease. The area rug is extremely portable, moving easily not only from room to room but from home to home as well. There is, of course, no installation cost involved in an area rug. Distributing the wear on such a rug is quickly and easily done. In addition, the bolder, more dramatically-designed area rug can also be hung on the wall for real versatility in a way that wall-to-wall could never match.

An area rug will leave a portion of your floor exposed. If that floor is in poor condition, with worn, uneven varnish or tile, such a rug would be a poor choice. If the floor is in good condition, it must be kept that way. That will mean cleaning, waxing and buffing around the rug. A word of warning: if you use an area rug on a bare floor, add double-faced tape to the underside to prevent slipping and sliding.

Of course, an area rug or two can be used to conceal worn spots in a wall-to-wall or room-size carpet. You must be careful in a cover-up operation like this to avoid creating a patched look or using little "scatter" rugs all over like steppingstones in a pond. That only draws attention to wear.

When deciding on the size of area rug to buy, you will find no hard-and-fast rule to follow. It is largely a matter of "looking right"—of keeping the rug in proportion to the room and the pieces surrounding it. However, if an area rug is to be used in a dining area, remember that all four chair legs should rest on the rug when the chairs are drawn back for use.

Many retailers are turning roll-ends and remnants into area rugs. Why not do the same? You can not only boast of your creativity, but can save dollars as well. Find a remnant you like in a size that suits your room, turn it over and, using chalk, draw the outline of the size and shape rug you want. Trim along the line, using a carpenter's square as a guide for your sharp knife. If the remnant is of woven construction or has a woven backing, you will probably have to bind the edges to avoid fraying.

When seeking a remnant, make sure that what you are considering is an "honest" remnant—that is, a leftover from a first-run carpet. Recently there has been an onslaught of stores springing up offering "seconds" and "remnants." These stores sell pieces of carpet manufactured to be sold as remnants at a low price. They also sell seconds—but do not label them as such. If you want a remnant, buy one from a reputable firm that is, in fact, selling remnant pieces from first-quality carpeting.

Area rugs come in all kinds of fibers and fabrics, as well as fur, skins and long, curly wool. Oriental rugs qualify as area rugs and are currently enjoying a resurgence of popularity for a variety of reasons. On the practical side, they wear very well, and their classic designs are timeless. In addition, they have, for some people, a mystical or symbolic lure. For others, the Oriental rugs' intricacy provides a nice complement to streamlined modern furniture, and still others see the rugs as financial investments. In fact, Raymond Albed, owner of the Albed Rug Company, specialists in Orientals and located along the Main Line area of suburban Philadelphia, reports that he believes his firm could do a significant business just in the carpet sold to agents from Germany and Japan. Albed says, "People in Europe and much of Asia have a great deal of money. They don't want to put any of it into currency because the market is very unstable. They don't like diamonds, and art has to be from the masters to appreciate in value.

"But you can always get at least what you paid for Persian rugs, and this is where many people in Europe and the Near East are putting money."

True Orientals are not for the budget-bound. As Jack Cox, who writes the "Carpet Wise" column for *Home Furnishings Daily*, says, "Prices of from $10 to $30 a square foot for the Chinese products, at retail, and from $10 to you-name-it for Orientals obviously mean a highly selective market."

These prices also mean that you had better know your Oriental carpets and your dealer. You're not dealing in brand names here with list prices for comparison shopping. If you plan to invest in one of these long-wearing beauties, read up on designs and construction before you go shopping. And when you are ready to shop, visit only reputable dealers. There are many rip-off artists in the Oriental rug business.

Selection is a strong point in favor of Oriental rugs. There are 440 types. The intricate designs and jewel-like colors plus the high prices have led many buyers to view the rugs as pieces of art too valuable to be walked on. Such rug fanciers hang the precious carpets on walls, drape them over sofa backs or even use them on tables.

Genuine Oriental rugs are handmade, using either the Ghiordes knot (Turkish) or the Senna knot (Persian). Those made with the Senna knot usually have a deeper, more uniform pile. Some of the fine old Orientals have as many as 500 knots per square inch. A good-quality modern rug could be expected to have about 200 knots to the square inch. Most of these long-wearing rugs are made of wool, although camel's hair and silk are used occasionally. There are, of course, machine-made copies of Oriental designs, and some of these are quite acceptable, as well as a great deal less costly than the originals.

Braided, hooked and needlepoint rugs are also common area rugs. The rya rug from Scandinavia is a deep shag usually in a striking design; it is hung on the wall almost as often as it is laid on the floor.

Area rugs may be had in wool, cotton, polyester and nylon in a variety of carpet weaves. This selection of fibers and weaves results in a wide spread of price levels for area rugs. You may buy a very inexpensive one or invest in what is really a work of art. For the average shopper, a good-quality area rug would be a wiser investment than cheap wall-to-wall.

ROOM-SIZE RUGS

A room-size rug is, quite obviously, just what the name implies. It is a carpet cut to fit your room. These rugs can be bought in standard sizes— 8 x 10, 9 x 12, 12 x 15, etc.—or you may have yours cut from roll carpet. Room-size rugs can be rolled and moved from apartment to apartment, from apartment to house with ease. If the rug proves too large for the next home, it is easily cut and bound. This is important to consider if you plan to move within a few years. Why waste money on a wall-to-wall installation you will have to leave behind?

If you wish to have a room-size rug cut from roll carpet, measure the length and width of your room to determine how much you will need. Most carpets come in 12- and 15-foot widths, and your rug will be cut from the standard width to the exact length you specify. For example, if your room measures 12 x 16-1/2 feet, you would order 16-1/2 feet of the 12-foot width. The rug would then completely cover the floor area. With a room measuring 14 x 17-1/2 feet, you would order 15-1/2 feet of the 12-foot width to get a rug leaving one foot of bare floor on all four sides.

Room-size rugs can be had in all fibers, weaves and patterns. They may be bought precut at prices starting from a low of around $15.95 for a 9 x 12 to a high of wherever-you-want-to-stop. Of course, for $15.95 you get a folded-up rug in a large plastic bag; in most cases, a coat of wax would be cheaper, better and probably last just about as long. Beware of the room-size rug that is just an oversized bathmat. A machine-washable 9 x 12 rug is a real problem—unless you own a laundromat. Even if you don't mind folding it, dragging it out to your car and hauling it to the giant washer and drier in the laundromat every few weeks, this should be considered as part of the cost of the rug. It may not be such a bargain, after all.

WALL-TO-WALL CARPETING

Finally, you may want to consider wall-to-wall carpeting—every year more and more people do. Wall-to-wall offers a luxurious appearance, creates an illusion of space and eliminates the need to clean and wax around the edges. However, it is not portable and cannot be turned to eliminate traffic wear.

Can you afford wall-to-wall carpeting? To answer that question, you must first know how much carpet you need. *Never* shop for wall-to-wall carpeting without knowing how much you need, and don't tell the salesman your estimate until he tells you his. Too many commission-counting salesmen will sell you yards you don't need—and then deliver only what you really require. For example, the salesman may tell you that you need 15 square yards. In truth, you need only 12 square yards. You pay for 15 square yards. He has only 12 delivered and relies on the fact that you won't measure the delivered piece.

Another trick is to write up a contract stating the amount you want to spend—10 square yards at $8.99 for a total of $899. "Great! That's even a dollar under my limit," you chirp happily. Great indeed, except that you need 14 square yards of carpet, will be delivered 14 square yards and will be charged for 14 square yards. Worse yet—the salesman only promised 10 square yards at $8.99. Any amount over the 10 yards may cost more per yard . . . plus padding, plus installation, plus, plus, plus.

To estimate square yardage, multiply the width of the room by the length—include both feet and inches. Don't round off 10 feet, 5 inches, to 10 feet. Divide your total by nine (there are 9 square feet in one square yard). This simple figuring will give you the square yardage of the area, but unless your room is exactly 12 or 15 feet wide (carpets are manufactured in these two widths), you will have to buy extra carpet and have it cut. Following is a table that converts feet and inches to square yards.

Don't stop figuring yet! Knowing your square yardage is basic, but not final. You may shop confidently, computing total yardages in your head with brisk efficiency, and then have the salesman befuddle you by computing your sale in running feet. Sears, Roebuck and Company, the ultimate foursquare American retailer, advertises its carpet prices by square yards and sells by running feet. One running foot of 12-foot-wide carpet equals one and one-third square yards. One running foot of 15-foot-wide carpet equals one and two-thirds square yards. Whether figured in square yards or running feet, the total amount of carpet and the total cost should be the same—unless a few extra running feet manage to scamper in while you are bewildered.

When totaling up your square yardage, plan to buy extra yardage for stairs. Have the extra folded against one or two of the risers at the top of the flight. Then, when the carpet begins to wear, you can shift the carpet downward, thus extending both its life and your investment.

SQUARE YARDAGE TABLE

1-100 Ft. Lengths
Feet and Inches Reduced to Square Yards

INCHES

Lineal inches	9' sq. yds.	12' sq. yds.	15' sq. yds.
1	.08	.11	.14
2	.17	.22	.28
3	.25	.33	.42
4	.33	.44	.56
5	.42	.55	.70
6	.50	.67	.84
7	.58	.78	.97
8	.67	.89	1.11
9	.75	1.00	1.25
10	.83	1.11	1.39
11	.92	1.22	1.53

FEET

Lineal feet	9' sq. yds.	12' sq. yds.	15' sq. yds.
1	1.00	1.33	1.67
2	2.00	2.67	3.33
3	3.00	4.00	5.00
4	4.00	5.33	6.67
5	5.00	6.67	8.33
6	6.00	8.00	10.00
7	7.00	9.33	11.67
8	8.00	10.67	13.33
9	9.00	12.00	15.00
10	10.00	13.33	16.67
11	11.00	14.67	18.33
12	12.00	16.00	20.00
13	13.00	17.33	21.67
14	14.00	18.67	23.33
15	15.00	20.00	25.00
16	16.00	21.33	26.67
17	17.00	22.67	28.33
18	18.00	24.00	30.00
19	19.00	25.33	31.67
20	20.00	26.67	33.33
21	21.00	28.00	35.00
22	22.00	29.33	36.67
23	23.00	30.67	38.33
24	24.00	32.00	40.00
25	25.00	33.33	41.67

FEET

Lineal feet	9' sq. yds.	12' sq. yds.	15' sq. yds.
26	26.00	34.67	43.33
27	27.00	36.00	45.00
28	28.00	37.33	46.67
29	29.00	38.67	48.33
30	30.00	40.00	50.00
31	31.00	41.33	51.67
32	32.00	42.67	53.33
33	33.00	44.00	55.00
34	34.00	45.33	56.67
35	35.00	46.67	58.33
36	36.00	48.00	60.00
37	37.00	49.33	61.67
38	38.00	50.67	63.33
39	39.00	52.00	65.00
40	40.00	53.33	66.67
41	41.00	54.67	68.33
42	42.00	56.00	70.00
43	43.00	57.33	71.67
44	44.00	58.67	73.33
45	45.00	60.00	75.00
46	46.00	61.33	76.67
47	47.00	62.67	78.33
48	48.00	64.00	80.00
49	49.00	65.33	81.67
50	50.00	66.67	83.33
51	51.00	68.00	85.00
52	52.00	69.33	86.67
53	53.00	70.67	88.33
54	54.00	72.00	90.00
55	55.00	73.33	91.67
56	56.00	74.67	93.33
57	57.00	76.00	95.00
58	58.00	77.33	96.67
59	59.00	78.67	98.33

EXAMPLE

62' 8" of 12 ft. width
62' - 82.67 sq. yds.
8" - .89 sq. yds.
total - 83.56 sq. yds.

FEET

Lineal feet	9' sq. yds.	12' sq. yds.	15' sq. yds.
60	60.00	80.00	100.00
61	61.00	81.33	101.67
62	62.00	82.67	103.33
63	63.00	84.00	105.00
64	64.00	85.33	106.67
65	65.00	86.67	108.33
66	66.00	88.00	110.00
67	67.00	89.33	111.67
68	68.00	90.67	113.33
69	69.00	92.00	115.00
70	70.00	93.33	116.67
71	71.00	94.67	118.33
72	72.00	96.00	120.00
73	73.00	97.33	121.67
74	74.00	98.67	123.33
75	75.00	100.00	125.00
76	76.00	101.33	126.67
77	77.00	102.67	128.33
78	78.00	104.00	130.00
79	79.00	105.33	131.67
80	80.00	106.67	133.33
81	81.00	108.00	135.00
82	82.00	109.33	136.67
83	83.00	110.67	138.33
84	84.00	112.00	140.00
85	85.00	113.33	141.67
86	86.00	114.67	143.33
87	87.00	116.00	145.00
88	88.00	117.33	146.67
89	89.00	118.67	148.33
90	90.00	120.00	150.00
91	91.00	121.33	151.67
92	92.00	122.67	153.33
93	93.00	124.00	155.00
94	94.00	125.33	156.67
95	95.00	126.67	158.33
96	96.00	128.00	160.00
97	97.00	129.33	161.67
98	98.00	130.67	163.33
99	99.00	132.00	165.00
100	100.00	133.33	166.67

Installation service

Wall-to-wall carpeting must be installed. Improper installation of wall-to-wall carpet is a common gripe heard by the Better Business Bureau. While do-it-yourself installation is possible in a small, square room, such as a bedroom, it is not a good idea for the average buyer to attempt to install wall-to-wall carpet in living, dining and hall areas. The proper sewing and placement of seams, considering the "lay" or "sweep" of the fiber, the wrapping of stairs and stretching for tight fit are all jobs for a professional. It is penny-wise, pound-foolish to buy good carpeting and then butcher it in an attempt to save installation costs.

In fact, a good installer can actually save the buyer money through his advice on such considerations as the proper weight for the pad, the evaluation of how temperature and humidity (important in below-street-level installations) will affect carpeting.

Many stores offer installation service, although the cost is increasingly burdensome. Often the retailer—particularly the carpet specialty store —makes a package price of carpet, pad and installation. Feelings are mixed on the fairness of such offers. The owner of a quality furniture chain in the Midwest advertises and prices carpet alone, not as a package with padding and installation included, because, "It's not fair to the customer. If she chose a $5 carpet, and the pad and installation run about $5 a yard, and we advertised it as a $10 carpet installed, she'd think she was getting a much better piece of goods than a $5 item."

If you do choose to buy a package deal, have the salesman itemize the cost of each included item. Check to see whether you are getting savings through the package or whether you would be better off to arrange for each item—carpet, pad and installation—separately.

If your carpet dealer does not have his own installer, he can direct you to one. As faulty installation can significantly reduce the wear- and life-expectancy of any carpet, it is well worth the time spent to find an experienced and capable installer. Find an installer with a good reputation. Ask for references that testify to the quality of his work, and check a few of them. Go out and inspect the actual installation.

You may be able to save significantly by contracting your own installation. A leading retailer in Pittsburgh says of installers, "We have one gripe. Some union installers have gone into competition with themselves by moonlighting—some of them at well under union scale rates and with good work. They are also in competition with their bosses and with us, their bosses' clients, or with their retail employers."

Whether you contract your installation independently, arrange it through your retailer or take a package deal, there are certain facts that should be checked. What kind of installation are you getting—tacked-down, tackless, double-faced tape, glue? Does the price include all seams? If not, how many? Is there a separate charge for stairs? Balcony overhangs? Are metal strips (thresholds) included in the price quoted? How about an extra charge for below-street-level installations? Does measuring cost extra?

Have everything spelled out and make the quoted price the total price. It's too late to object when the carpet is installed and the bill presented.

CARPET TILES

It is the cost and bother of carpet installation that have helped make rubber-backed carpet tiles so popular. Many carpet tiles are inexpensive and may be had in a variety of fibers and weaves, including shag. It must be said that too many carpet tiles are little more than lint on rubber. Also they are not always a bargain; in many cases you can carpet a room for the same price that you will pay for the best tiles.

Most often 12 inches square, but also offered in 9- and 8-inch squares, the tiles are easy to handle and usually have an adhesive backing. Generally offered for kitchen, rec. room or bathroom use—tough-wear areas— the tiles have been criticized because some users found that after repeated vacuumings, spills and shampoos, the corners tend to work up or tiles no longer align properly.

In fact, in off-the-record discussions salespeople and dealers often dismiss carpet tiles as "gimmicks" or "junk" beneath the attention of real carpet buyers and sellers. Certainly many dealers in good-quality floor coverings refuse to carry them, and those that do are not enthusiastic. As improvements are made in the quality of the tiles, this viewpoint will change. For now, however, carpet tiles are scornfully relegated to home centers and do-it-yourself departments.

COLOR AND PLANNED OBSOLESCENCE

Once a total buying price—covering all costs—and the type of rug or carpet to be bought have been determined, color can be considered. Remember, you can get just about any color at any price level.

For many years beige held the top color position for carpet. However, the carpet industry has worked very hard in the past few years to promote color—color to suit your every mood and desire. Exciting color, wild

Carpet tile calculator

Length \ Width	5	6	7	8	9	10	11	12	
5	45	54	63	72	80	89	98	107	9"
	25	30	35	40	45	50	55	60	12"
	12	14	16	18	20	23	25	27	18"
6	54	64	75	86	96	107	118	128	9"
	30	36	42	48	54	60	66	72	12"
	14	16	19	22	24	27	30	32	18"
7	63	75	88	100	112	125	137	150	9"
	35	42	49	56	63	70	77	84	12"
	16	19	22	25	28	32	35	38	18"
8	72	86	100	114	128	143	157	171	9"
	40	48	56	64	72	80	88	96	12"
	18	22	25	29	32	36	40	43	18"
9	80	96	112	128	144	160	176	192	9"
	45	54	63	72	81	90	99	108	12"
	20	24	28	32	36	40	44	48	18"
10	89	107	125	143	160	178	196	214	9"
	50	60	70	80	90	100	110	120	12"
	23	27	32	36	40	45	49	54	18"
11	98	118	137	157	176	196	216	235	9"
	55	66	77	88	99	110	121	132	12"
	25	30	35	40	44	49	54	59	18"
12	107	128	150	171	192	214	235	256	9"
	60	72	84	96	108	120	132	144	12"
	27	32	38	43	48	54	59	64	18"
13	116	139	162	185	208	232	254	278	9"
	65	78	91	104	117	130	143	156	12"
	29	35	41	47	52	58	64	70	18"
14	125	150	175	200	224	249	274	299	9"
	70	84	98	112	126	140	154	166	12"
	32	38	44	50	56	63	69	75	18"
15	134	160	187	214	240	267	294	320	9"
	75	90	105	120	135	150	165	180	12"
	34	40	47	54	60	67	74	80	18"

This chart is helpful in determing how many tiles are needed to cover a given area. To use the chart, measure the area to be covered, read across the table to room width, read down to room length. There are three numbers given. The first is for 9-inch tiles, the second for 12-inch tiles and the third for 18-inch tiles.

color, daring color, romantic color—you name it, there's a carpet color to suit it. And name it they do. An ad for Lees carpets offers "Have-a-Fling" shag carpet in Raja Red, Playful Pink, Blazer Blue, Misty Jade and 19 other zippy colors.

High-low cut shags dazzle with many different colors woven together. Geometric and floral designs are vivid, plaids are bold. Tweeds are tweedier than ever. Ethnics are definitely in—Navajo designs compete for attention with Chinese motifs. Solids are available in an ever-growing number of hues, with some manufacturers offering as many as 50 colors.

Why all the big razzmatazz push for color and pattern? Just to brighten your life? Hardly. Consumers are getting harder to please, but, more important, the brighter, more daring, more "today" color you choose, the more likely you are to replace it. It's the old concept that Detroit has made so popular—planned obsolescence. So-called creative floors are replaced much more quickly than noncreative ones. *Western Merchandiser*, a trade magazine, not long ago ran an article called "Rub Out Beige-Carpet Owners" in which W. B. Guinan, president of Karastan Rug Mills, hailed color and pattern in rugs as another ". . . step toward planned obsolescence in floor coverings. As newer and more exciting looks in rugs and carpets are introduced, it becomes possible to convince the homemaker that a new rug or carpet will brighten her home and her life, especially if she's still one of the thousands of beige-carpet owners." You see, people with beige carpet just don't replace it until it's threadbare. They get a lot of wear and service for their investment. The color works well with other colors, hides soil and wear, and doesn't make you want to put on sunglasses the minute you enter the room. After all, a three-foot swatch of "Sizzling Pink" may seem terrific in the showroom; 30 feet of the same color may lead to jangled nerves and damaged eyesight.

In his "Carpet Wise" column in *Home Furnishings Daily*, Jack Cox (a beige-carpet owner himself) advises retailers that ". . . the problem of getting the customer to think of carpet not as a once-in-a-lifetime purchase—or a product which should last 20 years on her floor—is probably one of the toughest the industry faces."

Color and pattern are the tools the industry is using to solve this problem. Their use, of course, pays off for the consumer in greater selection and more attractive and dramatic floor coverings. However, a cautious hand is recommended. In reply to the question "Which color should I buy?", Sears, Roebuck answers, "Just pick one you love . . . it's going to be around for a long, long time." Uh huh—like a husband. Make sure it's love and not a mere infatuation, not just a "surface" attraction. Make sure it's compatible, reliable—an all-occasion love, a love to last for many happy, satisfying years. Save your infatuations and flings for inexpensive area rugs that can be dropped when the thrill is gone.

For the past six or seven years, golds and greens have been the two dominant, best-selling colors in the carpet field. Earth tones and neutrals have always been strong sellers. Dorothy Liebes, one of the world's top fabric designers, once said, "In taking colors from nature, a designer is always on sure ground, for nature makes no aesthetic mistakes."

The color you choose should blend with existing furnishings and should suit the purpose of the room in which the carpet will be laid. That is, carpeting a family room in white shag would be foolish. Such a hard-wear area needs a more soilproof color. Dark colors, such as navy blue, also show soil quickly.

Whether or not the rug is going to a permanent resting place can also affect the choice of color. A young couple in an apartment may buy a living room rug with plans to use it in a bedroom in their first house. A neutral color is a safe choice for either use; give careful thought to versatility if you're considering a pattern or dramatic color.

There are advantages and disadvantages to patterned floor coverings. Patterns—not sculptured designs now, but multicolored patterns—tend to hide soil and wear and, therefore, may give longer service than a non-patterned carpet of the same fiber. However, they also tend to be more limiting in decorating than solid colors and thus may wear out their welcome before you wear out their fibers.

Printed carpets started life in the family room and kitchen. Technology and design techniques have combined to push prints over the threshold into living rooms, dining rooms and bedrooms. In mid-1974 prints were estimated to be taking 18 per cent of the broadloom market—and aiming for 25 per cent and beyond. There are those who predict that by 1980 half of all carpeting sold in the United States will be printed.

Prints are available in everything from conservative monochromatic patterns to hysterically-multicolored designs replete with slogans. With an eye to the long haul, the less hysterical the better.

FIND OUT WHAT IT'S MADE OF

Consumer-service groups and government agencies continually receive complaints regarding carpet wear. Of course, shoddy products must take the blame due them, but many of these complaints could have been avoided if shoppers had taken the time to learn something about carpet fibers and construction before buying. Don't expect to get the needed facts from the carpet salesperson. Chances are he won't know any more about fibers than you do.

Fiber should be chosen according to your specific needs. It is important to remember that there is no one "best" carpet. With today's selection of fibers and weaves, certain kinds of carpets are "best" for certain uses. Pick the fiber that best suits your needs.

Although there is a mind-bending number of fiber trade names and grades on the market, there are really only five basic types used extensively in today's carpet: wool, nylon, acrylic, polyester and polypropylene.

Wool

The cost of wool has recently placed it out of reach for many mills, and it has, as a result, declined steadily in use. It is quite expensive but is long-wearing, luxurious, lustrous and resilient. Wool takes color dyes wonderfully well, and truly jewel-like tones are offered in wool carpets. On the minus side, wool tends to pill and shed rather badly during the first few months of use. Of course, some people are allergic to wool, and this should be considered when choosing a fiber.

Nylon

Nylon has long been the dominant fiber in the carpet and rug industry. It is the strongest carpet fiber made, one of the least expensive, is easy to clean and is nonallergenic. A continuous-filament nylon yarn has minimized the problems of pilling, fuzzing and shedding. Nylon's resistance to abrasion is outstanding and it is mothproof and mildew-resistant. The most common complaint regarding nylon concerns static electricity. (A humidifier can probably relieve the electricity build-up. It generally does not become a problem unless the relative humidity drops below 40 per cent.)

Acrylic

This manmade fiber looks so much like wool that many people are unable to tell them apart . . . until they look at the price tag. Acrylic is much less expensive. This fiber also cleans more easily than wool and is hard to stain. It is not as tough as nylon, doesn't do well in high-traffic areas and does not work well in shag constructions. Acrilan, Creslan and Orlon are big names in the acrylic field.

Polyester

Polyester is a bulky fiber that is quite stain-resistant and offers bright, clear colors with a rich look. However, these bright colors tend to show dirt, and the yarn isn't as long-lasting as nylon and acrylics. In fact, there have been serious "walk-out" problems with this fiber, but the industry is working hard to correct them. The best-known brand names in polyesters are Kodel, Dacron III, Fortrel, and Encron.

Polypropylene

The polypropylenes are the most stain-resistant fibers of all and, for that reason, are best suited for use in the kitchen, family room and kids' room. Artificial baseball and football turf is polypropylene, so the fiber is obviously well suited for use on home patios and decks too. Poly-propylenes are usually used in hard-finish and closely-woven rugs. They are not luxurious in appearance or texture, suffer somewhat from pilling and fuzzing, and have a low melting point. In fact, though polypropylene is basically long-wearing, a quick scrape of a leather heel can cause enough friction to form a burn line. The olefins such as Herculon and Marvess are polypropylenes.

Each of the many fibers available for use in carpeting can turn up in a selection of carpet constructions. The performance of any fiber depends to some degree on the amount of fiber used, the quality of construction and its use. For example, fiber with poor resilience can do well in a low, dense construction. Also, fibers are often used in tandem—the weak qualities of one offset the strong qualities of the other. Olefins are blended with nylon for better texture; wool is blended with acrylic to bring down the price of wool while retaining its advantages. You should consider both the fibers used and the construction—together and separately.

When shopping and comparing, don't try to compare wool with nylon, for example, for price value. Compare for price only nylon with nylon, wool with wool, and so on.

HOW IS IT MADE?

The general rule to follow when examining carpet construction is "The deeper, the denser, the better." When you are considering a particular carpet, bend it with face side out so that you can see where the tufts penetrate the backing. The less space between tufts and between rows, the better. The depth is easy to feel by touch. Generally, the density is more important than depth for good wear.

If, when you check the density, the carpet grins at you . . . don't grin back. "Grinning" is a term used to indicate that the carpet backing can be seen between the rows of pile tufts. Bend away from you a corner of the carpet you are considering. If the carpet grins, the tufts are not dense enough to give good performance. A grinning carpet does not have the proper tuft-to-tuft support, and the pile will crush and mat quickly. Manufacturers have faced the carpet backing with a dyed nylon cap that matches the surface pile in an attempt to "erase" grinning. Such tactics mask the problem, but don't eliminate it. The grinning carpet still won't wear well.

If a carpet does grin, it is the primary backing that you see. Most carpets have two layers of backing—primary and secondary. The outer layer—the one that touches the floor—is the secondary backing; the inner layer, the primary backing. At one time most carpets had primary backings of jute, a natural fiber from India, but, as in many other manufacturing areas, synthetics have taken over. In 1972, 70 per cent of the primary backings were synthetic, only 30 per cent jute. Additionally, 40 per cent of secondary backings were also synthetic. A study on the carpet industry compiled by J. W. Tucker Associates reported, "New types with needlepunch nylon face and dyeable polypropylene are being offered. A continued replacement of jute by synthetics is indicated over the coming years." Jute is strong, long-wearing and economical, but is subject to rot and mildew—something to be considered if you live in a mildew-prone area. The synthetics are nonallergenic and moisture-proof, and therefore will not rot or mildew.

Many people mistakenly believe *broadloom* to be a particular fiber or weave of carpeting. In fact, some retailers like to advertise "all broadloom" or "100 per cent broadloom" carpets. This is utterly meaningless. The term "broadloom" refers to carpeting at least 54 inches wide. It is woven on a broad loom. The term implies no qualities or characteristics other than width.

Over 80 per cent of all carpeting made today is tufted. Woven carpets (Wilton, Axminster and velvet), however, contain more fiber, which gives some extra wear over tufted carpet of equal depth and density. Woven does cost more, though, and the added cost is usually not offset in equally greater wear.

Shag has been the "high-fashion" star of the early seventies, but many in the industry expect that star to fade quickly. It's another aspect of planned obsolescence. The long (two inches or more) shags are a nightmare to maintain if they receive any wear at all and are unthinkable in a foyer, in a hall or on a stairway. Simple vacuuming is not enough. Long shags must be vacuumed with a special attachment that reaches down into the fibers and raises them. In between vacuumings the rug must be raked—with the same amount of vigor that you would use to rake leaves. It's hard, discouraging work, and the first few steps across the rug flatten it all out again. Of course, if there are children—or messy eaters— in the family who will be dropping cookie crumbs and potato chips into the thick, lush shag, the maintenance problem grows worse. Long shags also seem to swallow up dropped earrings, contact lenses and rings with amazing alacrity. The old saying, "like finding a needle in a haystack," could well be updated to "like finding a contact in a shag rug." Closely-woven, short shags hide (but don't eliminate) dirt, wear well and do not mat as quickly—but they *do* mat.

Cut-and-loop shags are popular, but are expected to be a short-lived fad. C & L, as it is known in the industry, has been cut at various heights to give a striking sculptured look. However, patterns can—and do—walk out, and a few are even hard to walk on.

Neither shag nor C & L is a good investment for the buyer who expects ten to 15 years of wear from her carpet.

Plush (or velvet) weave carpets have a rich, even texture that shows colors well . . . and dirt too. Plushes resist crushing and matting, but have "shading" problems. Footprints show as a different shade—it's like rubbing velvet the wrong way. This weave works well in formal living and dining areas and adult bedrooms, but does poorly in high-traffic areas and on stairs.

Tip-sheared carpet is a low-level mix of loops and cut pile, but the result here is a one-level surface that offers better wear and resilience than a long shag or C & L.

Sculptured carpet has two levels of loops that produce a carved pattern. These carpets are very durable and wear well in high-traffic areas.

Level loop is a tightly-woven carpet that's quite strong. When the fibers have been given a tight twist in each strand, the carpet will wear well and resist marks and soil. This is the best choice for family rooms, children's rooms and high-traffic areas like halls and stairs.

Finally, you may encounter "commercial" carpeting as you shop. This term can be used in several ways and can be quite misleading. Most people assume that commercial carpet is extra strong and durable, for use in stores, theaters and restaurants. The term can refer to a thin, hard-surface, good-wearing carpet at a low price, but it might also indicate a special-purpose carpet—and that can cover a multitude of sins and excesses. The Home Furnishings Council advises, "Beware of this term, especially in so-called bargain advertisements." In the spring of 1973 a long list of bargain seekers in Kalamazoo, Michigan, complained to that state's attorney general's office that they had been taken. They had purchased so-called commercial carpet billed as being far superior in quality to ordinary residential carpet. In fact, it was vastly overpriced and inferior in quality.

STANDARDS FOR TODAY AND THE FUTURE

After four years of battling between the carpet industry and the federal government, the UM-44c Carpet Standard and Certification Program went into effect March 1, 1975. Damned or hailed—depending upon which side of the fence you're on—this government program is seen as one of the toughest dealing with home furnishings. The UM-44c standards apply to many aspects of carpet durability, flammability and colorfastness. However, these guides concern only carpet to be included in the mortgage insurance and low-rent programs of the Department of Housing and Urban Development and the Federal Housing Administration. In other words, the UM-44c standards will *not* apply to carpet you buy in retail outlets; it will apply to carpet *installed* in federally-insured single-family and multi-family houses, as well as such housing for the elderly, and nursing homes. Will the federal government extend its authority to all carpets? Many observers see such action in the future.

AT THE BOTTOM OF IT ALL

Foam-backed carpet has the cushion actually bonded to the carpet. Most of the carpet sold in Europe today is foam-backed, but here the market has been generally limited to the carpeting designed for use in kitchens, basements and rec. rooms. Foam-backed carpets are not deeply luxurious, but are economical—eliminating the cost of a cushion—are mildew- and mold-resistant and super for do-it-yourself installations.

A good-quality foam-backed carpet should give you many years of service. In a poor-quality carpet the foam backing may separate from the carpet itself, creating unsightly "bubbles." In early carpets of this kind the foam tended to crumble, but technological improvements in backings have almost eliminated this problem.

Unless you buy a foam-backed carpet, do buy padding—and remember to figure it into your total cost. Don't assume that since no one will see the pad, you can "get away with" a cheap one. As well as adding comfort, padding can make your carpet last longer and look better. You can actually upgrade an inexpensive carpet with top-quality padding. It also provides insulation against noise, heat and cold.

Too many shoppers tend to "drop out" once they have hurdled all the decisions necessary in buying carpeting. They want to buy a pad, any pad, just so they don't have to make any more decisions. Padding is going to cost money now and save money in the long run. So don't drop out; pay attention and get your money's worth.

There are three basic kinds of padding: felted hair, sponge rubber and polyurethane. Felted hair usually comes in a waffle construction and is a good heat insulator. But, of the three, this pad does soil and break most easily and is most likely to mold and mildew. Sponge rubber is the softest padding. It doesn't retain odors and is nonallergenic. Polyurethane is very bouncy, nonallergenic and moldproof.

Each of these materials is available in a wide variety of grades, and the best way to decide which you prefer is to try them. Place a sample of the carpet you have selected over the cushion on the floor and step on them. Be careful not to choose a pad so soft and bouncy that it "bottoms out." This "squooshy" feeling may seem luxurious—"Oh, I just sink in up to my ankles!"—but it would result in distortion that would shorten the life of your carpet.

The felted and rubber pads are sold by weight—the number of ounces per square yard. Get at least a 40-ounce pad no matter which type you choose. The polyurethane is sold on the basis of thickness and density—a one-inch pad will offer the comfort and durability most buyers desire.

If you are buying a package deal—carpet, pad and installation—be sure to check the pad quality and weight. The dealer often makes his profit by including cheap padding in such deals, assuming—usually correctly—that the buyer won't check.

SURVIVING SALES STRATEGY

Armed with a price list, a color choice and an understanding of carpet construction, you can confidently face even the most intimidating floor coverings store. As carpeting can be an expensive purchase that is expected to give many years of service, it is important to choose a reputable dealer who will offer first-quality carpeting backed up by a reliable wear guarantee and, if you wish, expert installation. In addition to the general rules to be followed when choosing a retailer (see Chapter 4), there are certain specifics that apply only to floor coverings dealers.

Certainly, top-quality dealers advertise sales, specials and package offerings from time to time. Watching for such dollar-saving events can lead to honest bargains, but be careful of ads offering: "All the beautiful broadloom carpeting you need for living room, dining room and hall. $399. No extras! This includes everything—installation and padding." Reputable dealers do make such offers. (They first check their records to determine their average installation and then determine the amount of yardage and/or price to be offered.) Unfortunately, a great many disreputable dealers also make such offers. Beware of the dealer who *constantly* promotes three or four rooms—or even a houseful—of carpeting for a "surprisingly" low price.

If you call the dishonest dealer for his "convenient shop-at-home" service (he probably doesn't have a showroom), you can expect a fasttalking, high-pressure salesman to arrive at your door with the news that this "surprisingly low-priced carpet" is available in only one or perhaps two colors—and those two colors may well be eggplant and puce. The purpose of most of these ads is to get a salesman into your home to convince you to buy a more expensive carpet. If you hold out for the advertised offer, it will probably be found that your rooms are not of the proper sizes to qualify for the offer. Your rooms will cost quite a bit more to carpet.

If you insist on buying the advertised carpet, the salesperson may indeed sell it to you and take your deposit—but don't count on ever receiving it. The sales contract most likely will not specify a time of delivery, making legal action difficult. When you protest, the salesperson will try to switch you to a better—read more expensive—carpet. Don't try to beat these shysters at their own game. Just stay away.

Although the FTC is trying to crack down on such tactics, most inhome shoppers answering such ads do buy—often because they are poor credit risks unable to buy through regular channels on "convenient budget plans."

A reputable dealer will have a place of business where you can see carpet samples. He will not do business on a door-to-door or telephonesolicitation basis *only*.

Of course, there are many legitimate sales and specials, and they are worth watching for. Generally, July and August are big months for carpet sales, but special promotions are interspersed throughout the calendar.

If you have gone to a particular store in response to an ad, be sure you don't fall prey to the old "bait-and-switch" routine. This deceptive gimmick has been unfortunately common in the carpet business and, despite legislation by the federal government and the efforts of industry groups, such as the Retail Floorcovering Institute, is still with us.

When you do go to the store of your choice, expect an enthusiastic greeting. Retailers just love to sell carpeting. It is not only what is called a "big ticket" sale—meaning in the hundreds of dollars—but it offers the retailer the bonus of requiring no touch-ups, polishing or careful inspection before delivery. Also, when installed, new carpeting often tends to make old furniture look older and is a foot-in-the-door for new home furnishings purchases.

A competent salesman should immediately determine your needs in terms of price, color and fiber. He may, of course, show you samples at the price you specify and then attempt to entice you into a more expensive floor covering through persuasive salesmanship. More likely, however, he will start by showing you the top of the line, lauding benefits and features without ever mentioning price. Reasonably enough, you may assume that the samples being praised are at the price level you specified. Research has shown that, following this approach, the customer will very often step herself up to the top-priced line. Often price is not mentioned until the yardage is being figured and the total cost tallied. At this time the customer is often reluctant to back off and makes the purchase for many dollars over her budgeted limit.

You have established a limit after careful consideration. Stick to it. If you are really sorely tempted to spend more than planned, go home and think it over away from the desired carpet and the persuasive salesman.

Make it clear to the salesman that you have informed yourself on fibers and carpet construction. Ask questions and keep asking them until you get satisfactory answers. Home furnishings salesmen have long been instructed to sell beauty, status, luxury and other intangible benefits, ignoring the basic wear features.

SWATCHES STOP SWITCHES

When you have chosen the carpet and pad that you prefer at the price you want to pay, make sure you get a sample of each. A reputable dealer will be happy to provide you with these swatches. If your salesman assumes an indignant attitude or acts insulted by your request, think twice about the purchase. Those swatches could protect you from a nasty switch. (Copying down manufacturers' code numbers is not much help. Labels are easily switched.)

Most manufacturers produce carpets similar in appearance and color, but different in quality. For example, a given carpet may be available in three grades of pile—one more dense and expensive than the next. You may purchase the most expensive grade. Then, if your dealer is not honest, he can deliver the cheapest grade. He counts on the fact that it has been several days since you saw the carpet you selected, and once it is installed it will be difficult to prove the difference.

So get that swatch. When your carpet is delivered, check it carefully against the swatch. The same switch can be applied to padding, so check that too. Check both *before* installation.

BEFORE YOU SIGN IT

You will have several options when you discuss paying for your floor covering. These options are covered in Chapter 9. There are, however, some considerations unique to contracts for carpeting. Whether you pay cash or pay in installments, read your sales contract carefully to make sure it includes:

1. A description of the fiber by weight.
2. A description of the carpet weave.
3. Carpet color—with code number.
4. A statement to the effect that your carpet passes government flammability tests.
5. Exact yardage and price per yard of both carpet and pad.
6. Installation fee and any installation extras.
7. Total price, less your down payment.
8. Guarantees regarding wear, colorfastness and shrinkage.

AFTER YOU'VE GOT IT ON THE FLOOR

If, after all the careful preparation and wise shopping, you decide, on seeing the carpet on your floor, that you have made a mistake in terms of color or pattern, what can you do about it? Certainly, if you have an area rug or a ready-cut room-size rug, you should have no difficulty obtaining a refund or exchange. Many retailers will *exchange* wall-to-wall carpeting; they may not offer a refund. The carpet has, after all, been cut and seamed especially for your room.

Installation of wall-to-wall carpeting is often guaranteed for a stated period of time, with defects to be corrected without charge. Many dealers also offer a wear guarantee which states the number of years both the carpet and pad are guaranteed for. If the carpet fails to meet the established standards, the dealer may replace it at a stated prorated cost.

All guarantees and service statements should be made clear at the time of purchase. Don't wait until you have stretch ripples waving across your living room to ask if your installation is guaranteed. Have all guarantees spelled out. No reputable dealer will hesitate to do so. In fact, a good dealer is usually proud of his service and makes it a conspicuous part of his sales effort.

NINE

Paying for It
and Living
Happily Ever After

You have shopped carefully and found good furnishings at the price you want to pay. Now—how do you want to pay? The fact that over 260 million credit cards are in active circulation doesn't mean you can't go ahead and pay good, old-fashioned cash. It's simple, direct and most economical. If you pay cash, you're going to save credit service charges and interest; you won't have to worry about making monthly payments; you can plan for other purchases more freely. Finally, you don't have to go through the hassle of filling out credit applications and checking out the contracts.

Probably the retailer would much prefer to have you buy on time because of the cash profit to him on the financing, and the salesperson may well try to hustle you into signing up for the store's charge card. Remember: most home furnishings are big-ticket purchases. If you charge and don't pay it off immediately (and if you do, why charge it?) you're going to pay interest charges. Again—if you can pay cash, do so.

Another plus for paying cash came about as a result of a suit filed by Consumer's Union. In 1974 the American Express Company agreed to authorize merchants accepting its credit cards to grant 6 per cent discounts to cash customers. Other major credit card companies are expected to follow American Express' lead.

When you pay cash, remember to keep all your receipts marked PAID, in case you have to request an exchange, return or service. It's a good idea to keep your canceled check as a further record of your purchase.

"But," you protest, "if I charge it, I can have it now and I can buy more at one time." True, there are advantages to buying on credit: you can enjoy the use of your purchase while you're paying for it; you can take advantage of sales when you don't have ready cash; your home can be furnished more quickly if you avoid waiting until you have saved enough to pay cash. When you buy home furnishings on credit, you are essentially buying *time*, in that you use your *future* income to satisfy your wants *now*.

Even though ads urge you to "Add to your buying power. Use our E-Z payment plan," credit really does not give you greater power. Poorly-used credit cuts down on your buying power because after you pay finance charges, you have less money left over to spend. As the Better Business Bureau says in its publication "Consumer Tips on Buying on Time," "You always pay more for something if you buy it on time rather than pay cash for it."

Before you decide to buy your home furnishings purchase on credit, ask yourself: Can I wait to save up a bigger down payment? Can I make the payments—plus all my other monthly payments? Will I have money left over to cover emergencies? Is the item worth the extra cost of credit?

If you answer all the questions affirmatively and decide to buy on credit, you certainly will not be alone. In 1970 the average consumer was plunking down 60 cents out of every dollar to installment, noninstallment and mortgage debts. Over 80 per cent of all home furnishings purchases are made on credit.

Retailers love to sell on credit. *Some home furnishings dealers make no profit at all on the furniture they sell—just on the financing for that furniture.* Others happily profit on both the furniture and the financing. Of course, you must reasonably expect to pay for credit. The object of the game is not to pay any more than you have to . . . and certainly not more than you know about.

TRUTH-IN-LENDING LAW

Since 1969 you have had the federal Truth-in-Lending law to help you get a clear explanation of terms and costs when buying on credit. This law, introduced by Senator Paul Douglas of Illinois in 1960, was a landmark in this country's consumer protection action. The fight for the bill's passage was a long and bitter one. Retailers, finance companies, bankers, car dealers all fought against it with fierce dedication. The head of the National Retail Merchants Association called the bill "unrealistic, misleading and dangerous."

What unrealistic rights does this "dangerous" law give the consumer? Basically, the Truth-in-Lending law provides that the credit buyer must be told the true dollar amount of finance charges—total cost of credit including interest, service and carrying charges, any charges for required insurance, and (here's the part that upset the opposition) the *annual* percentage rate.

The law doesn't regulate the rate which may be charged; states do that. It just says you must be told what the rate is. Money-lenders and credit institutions like to offer credit on a monthly basis because their charge seems to be tiny when expressed that way. For example, the annual percentage rates for typical monthly rates are the following.

Rate per month	Annual percentage rate
¾ of 1%	9%
1%	12%
1¼%	15%
1½%	18%
2½%	30%

When you compare the cost of credit from various lenders, be sure to do the comparing in terms of annual percentage rate.

You will find that many home furnishings and department stores apply the 18 per cent annual rate. This rate has been outlawed in some states and is being questioned in several more. In 1974 Sears, Roebuck discontinued credit promotions in five states when those states lowered the finance charge ceiling below 18 per cent. Spiegel pulled out of the mail-order business in Wisconsin when that state lowered its limit to 12 per cent. If these big stores watch the annual percentage rate so closely, can you afford not to?

Despite the Truth-in-Lending law, loan contracts still blur the true annual percentage rate with legal jargon; but the facts are in there, and the law says they have to be conspicuously printed. It's up to you to look for them, ask about them and understand them. Also, too many people still concentrate on the amount of the monthly payment and let the total take care of itself. Of course, your monthly payment must be an amount you can afford, but don't let that amount blind you to other costs.

DASHING INTO DEBT

Home furnishings can be bought on a variety of credit plans—some better than others. Most shoppers, it has been found, have hang-ups about getting into complicated credit arrangements, so if a retailer has his own credit plan and handles all arrangements without delay, the shopper just signs up without looking into other plans elsewhere. While terms vary greatly, it may be possible to save on interest and service charges by obtaining credit at your bank, credit union or savings-and-loan association. You may have a credit card that offers better terms than those given by the furniture store. The home furnishings dealer doesn't have any corner on credit plans that are loaded with interest charges, service fees, minimum monthly payments and catch clauses. Abuse in these areas has been dismally commonplace, and both state and federal governments have been forced to pass legislation protecting the credit buyer. However, because your home furnishings purchase will probably run into hundreds of dollars with proportionately high credit costs, you should learn as much as possible about credit.

Revolving credit plans

Revolving credit or charge accounts, continuous credit plans, open-end credit are all essentially the same thing. Revolving credit combines monthly repayments with an open-end charge agreement. The Truth-in-Lending law defines revolving or open-end credit as credit extended under an agreement which permits the consumer to make additional purchases from time to time; gives the consumer the option of paying the balance in full or in installments; and permits a finance charge to be levied monthly (or periodically) on the outstanding unpaid balance.

Revolving plans are used by all kinds of retail operations, department stores and credit-card companies. The interest charges are profitable to the lender, and the plans encourage you to buy more through the ease of adding-on without fuss. For this reason they are heavily promoted and every effort is made to convert cash customers into revolving-charge-account buyers. Some of the advertising copy merits translation: "No down payment"—true enough, but the finance charge is higher because you finance a larger amount; "Lower monthly payments"—you pay less per month, but you pay longer, with a resulting higher credit charge;

"Liberal credit policy" probably means they'll take a greater risk but will charge you more for it; "Convenient monthly statement" is not a kindly courtesy but is required by federal law.

Even though the revolving credit plan is a real gravy-maker for the retailer, there are gimmicks used to thicken that gravy. Many home furnishings dealers figure monthly service charges on the previous month's ending balance. That is, they compute their charges *before* subtracting the monthly payment, instead of after. To see how this works, compare Store Top-Profit, which computes its charges before subtracting the monthly payment, with Store Fair-Deal, which computes after. A consumer who pays half of a $200 balance in the first month at Store Top-Profit will be charged 1-1/2 per cent of $200. The charge at Store Fair-Deal will be 1-1/2 per cent of $100. So, even though both charge 1-1/2 per cent on the "unpaid balance," the consumer's bill can be much higher at Store Top-Profit.

Consumer groups have been complaining for years about the previous-balance method and many lawsuits have been filed to test the issue. Most of the time the stores have won these cases, but, largely as a result of consumer protest, many creditors—led by Sears, Roebuck & Co. in 1972—have given up this method and have adopted the average-daily-balance method.

The average-daily-balance method seems to be fair to both the consumer and the creditor, although the creditor makes less profit by it. Under this system, each day's balance is figured by taking the previous day's balance and subtracting today's payments and credits. These balances are averaged for the month and the finance charge is based on that average.

The federal government does require all those who do not deduct payments before computing charges to state that fact on both the contract and the bill.

Open-end contracts usually give the dealer title to all merchandise until the last payment is made. Under this system you could pay for 90 per cent of the merchandise you charged and still lose it all. For example, using the add-on privilege, you may first buy a sofa for $500. After you reduce this balance to $30, you add on a pair of chairs for a total of $300. You continue to make your payments and have only one to go. That payment is late. The dealer can repossess both sofa and chairs, even though the sofa is paid for.

You can, though, make the plan work for you. Al Griffin in *The Credit*

Jungle (Regnery Company, 1971) says, "Anybody with a revolving charge account who really wants to enrage a banker or credit manager can do so quite simply by paying his bills *on time*. They all offer an interest-free 10- or 15-day grace period for payment of the bill before tacking on service charges. They don't actually want anybody to use it, and the bank card plans would quickly go broke if they didn't get their 18 per cent interest per year. A too-prompt payer is thus likely to be more unwelcome as a client than is a too-slow payer." You may not always be able to swing paying off a major home furnishings purchase in the free period allowed to you, but whenever you can, it's a wise move.

Nonrevolving plans

Everything other than revolving or open-end credit is referred to in the Truth-in-Lending law under the all-purpose term "other than open-end" credit. *Installment plans* are sheltered under the "other-than" umbrella—and the very fact that they don't even rate a category of their own shows how low they've sunk in the time-payment world. Installment plans have been shoved out of the limelight by the more profitable open-end plans which make it easier for the customer to keep adding on purchases and extend payments over a longer period of time—thus increasing finance charges. Installment credit is usually granted for one large purchase and is repaid in equal monthly installments over a set period of time. The customer gets hit with the total finance charges at the time credit is extended. If the customer wants to make another purchase before the first is paid off, he has to go through a credit interview all over again.

Installment plans carry an annual percentage rate of interest based on the actuarial method (or United States Rule), which must be plainly disclosed on the credit contract. With this method, on a $100 installment purchase, for example, a finance charge of $10 to allow the customer to pay off the debt in 12 equal monthly payments amounts to an actuarial annual percentage rate of 18 per cent . . . not 10 per cent, as you might assume.

Lay-away plans don't come under the Truth-in-Lending law if the retailer gives you the option of canceling the purchase and getting a prompt refund of any payments you may have made. He is entitled, however, to keep some compensation for the service of laying the merchandise away.

It is still possible to find stores that will offer 30-, 60- or 90-day installment contracts. Under these contracts, if you pay within no more than four installments, no carrying charges will be added to your total—"same as cash." You may be asked to pay the carrying charges at the time you sign the contract; these charges will be refunded if you pay within the stated time. Such deals are growing increasingly rare, however, as the retailer does not make the interest-profit on them that he does on revolving credit.

A not-so-pretty balloon

In many states the "balloon contract" is still legal. Don't sign one. Under the balloon contract the monthly payments are usually quite small, but the last payment balloons to outrageous dimensions. The last payment can actually be for hundreds of dollars, and if you can't pay it, you face repossession or garnishment or both.

Insuring the deal

Whether you want it or not, you may be required by the retailer to buy life insurance in order to finance your home furnishings purchase. The cost for this required insurance, which will pay off the account balance in the event of death, must be included as part of the finance charge—not as part of the amount being financed. There is no need to pay finance charges on that too.

If the credit life insurance is optional and you decide to take it, you should be able to pay for it separately if you wish. However, if it's not required, don't take it. Even if the insurance cost is only, say, fifty cents a month, that comes to $6.00 a year—or $18 if you take 36 months to pay. This is not a good insurance buy for you, but is super profit for the retailer.

Ask questions

If a store offers more than one credit plan—and many do—or if you are considering more than one source of credit, make sure you understand each plan before you make your decision. Ask questions and keep asking until you are sure you understand. Don't be fuddled by legal jargon or financial terminology; get it translated. Ask who you will make your payments to. Some stores turn over their credit "paper" to banks or finance companies. If this is the case, find out who is responsible for damaged goods and service. Find out what happens if you can't pay on time—will your purchase automatically be repossessed? If you pay ahead of time, will you be penalized . . . or will you get a refund on interest charges? Can you refinance if an emergency makes it impossible for you to make the monthly payments? If you do refinance, how will the balance be refigured?

Signing on the dotted line

When you do choose a credit plan, you're going to have to sign a contract, and once you do, you'll be legally and financially responsible for everything on that contract. (The Truth-in-Lending law gives you the right to cancel the contract within three days *only* if you have signed over a security interest in your house or some other type of real estate. In some states, sales made in the home are also subject to cancellation within three days.) Signing with only initials or a nickname won't exempt you from legal responsibility; even an *X* mark could hold up in court. Therefore, make sure you read and understand everything on the contract—front and back. If you don't understand it, don't sign it. The salesperson will no doubt be very reassuring and, if you continue to balk, gradually grow condescending or annoyed. If you ask to take the contract home with you or to bring an adviser in, the salesperson will most likely try to dissuade you from any such delay in signing. This pressure need not indicate that he is a gyp-artist trying to stampede you into a deceptive contract. He may simply be trying to nail down a sale and commission. Nonetheless, stand firm.

You may consult your attorney, an obliging banker or a knowledgeable friend for advice on the contract. You may also call your state's attorney's office for information on a specific question, but you are not likely to get an entire contract reviewed and approved. Unfortunately, some of the very people who most need help regarding contracts—non-English-speaking individuals or those with limited educations—are least likely to get it. When an assistant state's attorney in Illinois was asked where an individual who was unable to understand a contract could go for help, he replied, "Really nowhere, except to an attorney." When it was protested that many people couldn't afford an attorney's services, the answer was an abrupt "If they can't afford a lawyer, they shouldn't be buying anything anyway." He went on to explain that the local bar association might refer an individual with a bewildering contract to a lawyer who would "probably try to convince them that they needed his services to handle the deal—at a price."

One of the basic rules for financial survival—like "Look both ways before crossing the street"—is "Never sign a contract with spaces left blank." Contracts may take some time to fill out, but don't fall for "Just to save some time, why don't you sign these while I start processing your order. We can fill them in later." If there are blanks "that don't apply to you," fill them with large X marks before you sign. The salesperson won't object if they really don't apply to you.

Be sure the contract states:
Exactly what you are buying—manufacturer's name and model number—plus fabric grade code if you are specially ordering upholstered goods;

The price of the item you're buying;

Shipping charges, delivery or setup fees;

The amount of your cash down payment or trade-in allowance, if any;

The dollar amount of credit, interest and service charges;

The annual percentage rate;

The total amount to be paid;

The amount, number and due date of each payment;

The penalties for late payments;

The grace time allowed before repossession;

All promises made by the salesperson.

Verbal promises made by the salesperson are worthless. You are legally bound by what the contract says, not by what the salesperson has told you. If you are told the merchandise you are buying is returnable, have it put in writing. If you are told you can cancel your order if it is not delivered within, say, 60 days, have it added to the contract. Get all guarantees in writing.

Similarly, cross out words and phrases that don't apply to you. For example, if the salesperson has promised you full refund privileges if you are not satisfied with your purchase, but the contract allows returns only for exchange, not refund, delete the clause in the contract and add your own.

Make any deletions or additions on all copies. Read and check all copies that you are asked to sign—not just the top copy. The carbons could be different. Finally, get a fully-signed and dated copy of the agreement for yourself.

Fair Credit Reporting Act

When you apply for credit to buy your home furnishings, the retailer will most likely turn to a credit-reporting bureau for your credit rating. These bureaus, or consumer reporting agencies, as they are also called, are privately operated businesses that gather and sell credit information on consumers to various kinds of businesses, employers and insurers. This credit information can concern your character, popularity with your neighbors and lifestyle, as well as your bill-paying habits. Your file may also indicate whether or not you have ever been arrested or sued or have filed for bankruptcy.

Since April 1971, when the Fair Credit Reporting Act became effective, you have had the right to request the credit reporting agency to disclose the nature of the information reported on you. If you are denied credit, the retailer must give you the name of the firm that furnished the credit information against you. Within 30 days of being denied credit because of this information, the reporting bureau must disclose this information to you free of charge; if you have not been denied credit but are simply curious, expect to pay a fee to see your file.

If you wish to check on your file, you may locate the credit reporting bureaus in your community by consulting the telephone directory "Yellow Pages."

The Federal Trade Commission has established the Bureau of Consumer Protection (see Chapter 10 for address), and it is this bureau that enforces the Fair Credit Reporting Act. The implications of the act extend beyond consumer rights into the complex civil rights area. If you wish to challenge any information in your file, initiate a more thorough investigation or enter into a dispute with the credit reporting bureau, you would do well to get some professional legal advice.

If the bureau gives you a bad rating, you'll probably be refused credit—or you will have to come up with a big down payment, a co-signer or some kind of collateral.

DELIVERY

The type of store you are buying from will, to some extent, determine the kind of delivery you can expect. (The wait for delivery, of course, has been discussed earlier and will depend upon whether or not your item is a special order, is a shipment from the factory or from a local warehouse, or is a floor sample.) The full-service store will probably include unpacking, setup and placement in your room in its delivery service—and you generally will find that no extra charge is made. In the wake of the success of warehouse-showrooms, many stores are modifying their delivery policies, and it's advisable to ask just what delivery includes. To-the-door delivery may be free, with the other services available at a price. The warehouse-showroom and discount operations, of course, encourage you to haul your purchase yourself.

Don't get rid of your old furniture before the new arrives and is found satisfactory. Even if it means crowding the new in with the old for a day or two, it's better than being left sitting on the floor for months while the store reorders your sofa in the *right* color.

When your home furnishings are delivered, ask the delivery men to wait while you make a quick check. First, check model numbers and check for any optional extras you may have ordered. (See Chapter 8 for specific check points on carpet). The piece you inspected so carefully in the store is not the one you get at home—unless you bought a floor model, and even that could have been damaged in transit. In addition to looking for delivery-incurred damage, check the piece to make sure it is as well made as the one you saw on the store display floor. On casegoods, check the finish, drawers, doors and wood grain, just as you did in the store. On upholstered goods, check the fabric, color and pattern matching, and general construction. If you bought a suite, make sure all the pieces match. The retailer should have made a careful inspection before delivering the item to you, making any touch-ups and adjustments needed. Truly the retailer is virtually helpless regarding the depressing delays in delivery from the manufacturer and the damage incurred in shipping, and these are constant complaints in the industry. Such damage adds to his operating costs, drives up your purchase price and, not least important, results in unsatisfactory merchandise. A dab of varnish can't do much for a broken leg or dented dresser.

SATISFACTION GUARANTEED OR . . . WHAT?

After your first quick inspection while the delivery men wait, give your newly-delivered purchase a careful, thorough examination. Inspect all construction details for flaws. Study the piece in relation to your room. Does it look as you thought it would? Is it harmonious with the other furnishings and colors in the room? If you are in any way dissatisfied, notify the retailer immediately. Generally speaking, the more time you let lapse between delivery and your complaint or request for adjustment, the less chance you stand of success.

Among all the purchases you can make, furniture and carpeting are real complaint-bait. Robert W. Beghtol, manager of the home furnishings department of the New York Metropolitan Better Business Bureau, states that furniture is the number-one source of consumer complaints. As consumerism has gained momentum, complaints regarding home furnishings have increased—not because the merchandise has gotten worse, but because consumers have become more aware of their rights. Virginia Knauer, the Special Assistant to the President for Consumer Affairs in Washington, reported in 1974 that consumer complaints had shown strong gains in 1972, with furniture complaints pegged at a 29.2-per-cent gain over those logged in for 1971, and carpets and flooring complaint totals climbing 24.3 per cent over those of the previous year. "Consumer Help," a local television show in Washington, D.C., annually received several thousand complaints of all kinds. The home furnishings complaints sent to this show most often concerned: failure to deliver the merchandise as promised; shoddy merchandise; misrepresentation in advertising or warranty terms; refusal to return the customer's deposit if merchandise is not available, if credit is refused or if the customer will not be "switched" to higher-priced merchandise; and, finally, delivering the floor model—but charging the "new" price for it.

Most often, consumers complain about fabrics wearing out almost instantly, and tearing at seams and buttons. They report on lumpy mattresses and mattresses that bleed on the sheets. Wood-stain bleeding on the carpet and carpets that fade, shed or mat are other complaint producers. Improper installation and substitution of a lower grade than paid for are still other frequent carpet complaints.

Speaking out

If you have a complaint, make it. Ralph Charell, world champion complainer according to *The Guinness Book of World Records* (Bantam Books, Inc., 1974) and author of *How I Turn Ordinary Complaints Into Thousands of Dollars*(Stein & Day, 1973), says, "Everybody has to break the psychological habit of taking whatever is dished out to him. Grumbling isn't going to do anybody a bit of good—but complaining, to the right people, is one way of defending yourself against the poor goods and services most consumers accept meekly."

Complaints are not only negative, you know. On the positive side, a complaint tells a retailer or manufacturer how to improve his service or product; it helps prevent the same thing from happening to the next guy; it can draw attention to a needed consumer protection measure; and certainly it can get you what you paid for in the first place.

Get your facts straight before presenting them to the seller. Know exactly what you ordered and what service you were promised—in writing. Have names, dates and model numbers ready. Be able to express your complaint clearly, without a lot of needless detail, hysteria or hostility. Most likely this isn't some small purchase that you can toss in the back seat and drive to the store. You're going to have to convince them to come and get it.

What can you expect from the retailer? Of course, some dealers have built their reputations on liberal return and exchange policies, while others have done just the reverse. If you went for rock-bottom price or instant delivery at the time of purchase and cast postdelivery satisfaction to the winds, you may well regret it now. Service limitations, exchange and return policies should be clearly spelled out at the time of purchase. If you agreed to a no-return or no-refund policy—or one limited by a number of hours or days—don't expect the store to exceed that stated policy now. You took a chance and lost.

If however, the store pledged satisfaction and you are within your rights, make your complaint.

Be courteous. If you have waited months for delivery only to have the wrong item arrive, you are understandably upset, but screaming and swearing at the store representative will not help matters. Be willing to discuss the problem in detail—rationally. Find out what can be done, how long it will take and whether a fee will be charged. Get the name and department of the individual handling your complaint and write it down. Knowing that name can make follow-up calls more efficient.

If you request a full refund, chances are you'll be offered a replacement instead. If you refuse this offer, the store will likely next offer a "due bill" or "credit" which you can spend in the store—"just as good as cash." The due bill is as good as cash for the store, but not for you. If you don't want the due bill, and your sales contract does not specify otherwise, hold out for cash. Be assertive.

If you are within the rights of your sales agreement, don't be intimidated. A full refund will cost the salesman his commission; any replacement will cost the store money in terms of service. You will, therefore, likely find that warm, friendly salesman will turn somewhat frosty.

"I won't pay for it!"

In his book *Consumer Purchasing* (Pendulum Press, Inc., 1973), Robert W. Randall advises, "Do not pay the entire bill at the time of purchase. When your furniture arrives, inspect it while the delivery men are still there, because complaints should be made immediately. Don't make the final payments until you are satisfied." You might work this strategy to your advantage if you are paying cash and haven't signed a binding contract demanding payment on delivery—no matter what. However, if you are buying on credit, withholding payment will only bring additional interest charges and worse. The FTC is considering legislation that would permit you to stop payment on unsatisfactory merchandise financed on credit, but as things stand, you do not have that option. If you refuse to pay, you can be hauled into court and your purchase could be repossessed.

What about my guarantee?

Without going into hair-splitting legal jargon, there is no important difference between a guarantee and a warranty. They are both statements which are given to you at the time of sale and which set forth certain quality or performance standards and promise some specific action such as repair, replacement or refund if the product fails to meet the stated standards.

The law doesn't demand that either retailers or manufacturers must warrant their products. However, as of July 4, 1975, any warranties that are issued on products retailing for over $10 must meet certain federal standards. Such a warranty must be either "full" or "limited." A "full" warranty must promise repair, replacement or refund to remedy defects. All other warranties must be identified as "limited."

Most home furnishings manufacturers have not concerned themselves with issuing warranties—and those that have been issued usually don't cover much. No matter what the product, most warranties are written to limit the responsibility of the manufacturer—or at least to try to limit it. Many warranties for upholstered goods refuse to cover "normal" wear; others will warrant only those products which have received "normal" use and maintenance. Obviously, "normal" is an arguable term and a convenient out for the manufacturer.

Before relying on any warranty regarding your home furnishings purchase, read it carefully. Certainly, it should state *who* is making the warranty (Usually the firm offering the warranty is responsible for carrying out its promises—but not always. You can be bounced back and forth between the retailer and the manufacturer "like a ping-pong ball," as one store-owner described it); *to whom* it is offered; *what* is covered —product and parts; and for *how long.* This length of warranty is of particular concern regarding furniture; for example, springs, filling materials and casters may be covered for five years, but fabric for only one year. Also, if a lifetime warranty is offered, find out whose lifetime is involved—yours, the product's or the manufacturer's.

Your warranty should also clearly state *what the warrantor will do* to honor it and *what you must do.* If you have to bear the responsibility and cost of getting the furniture back to the manufacturer, you may find it both easier and more economical to simply hire a craftsman to come in and make the needed repairs. One large manufacturer warrants that he will bear the expense of transporting the furniture from the dealer back to his plant. But will the dealer bear the cost of getting it from your home to his store? That's up to you to find out; it's not in the warranty.

Finally, it can be as important to find out *what is excluded* from a warranty as it is to know *what is included.* Excluding labor costs, for example, is quite common. Holding a company responsible for an excluded service can be more difficult than if there were no warranty at all.

There's no escaping it: The best warranty is made by using care in making the purchase itself.

Who cares?

If you take your complaint to the store that sold you the merchandise and fail to get help or satisfaction, what next? You can try the manufacturer; however, even retailers have a difficult time getting satisfactory adjustments from manufacturers. Unless you're dealing with a consumer-oriented firm (and more and more are), you will not meet with success.

Don't give up yet. There are many agencies and organizations responsive to consumer problems. Motivated partly by a desire for better consumer relations and partly by fear that if the industry doesn't do something, the government will, groups of manufacturers have established special panels to answer consumer complaints. There are also local, state and federal agencies established to help.

When you write to one of these sources, send *copies only* of bills, contracts, letters and other documents. State your case clearly and concisely.

Two industry-established panels you may try are the following: Furniture Industry Consumer Advisory Panel and Carpet and Rug Industry Consumer Action Panel (see Chapter 10 for addresses). Because both were formed in 1974, it is not possible to judge their effectiveness on such slim track records. However, since they are creations of the very forces that have long opposed consumerism, it will be surprising if they become strong arbitration sources.

There are well over 100 Better Business Bureaus across the country, and you may wish to register your complaint with the one nearest you. If the dealer involved in your complaint is reputable, he may wish to reply to the Better Business Bureau; however, he doesn't have to. The bureau does not have the authority to take any action against him.

Arbitration is a fairly new service offered by most Better Business Bureaus. It is free and, in most cases, binding under the law. Arbitration has proved very effective in cases where the consumer and the business involved could not agree on the facts. Going to court to resolve the issue is both expensive and time-consuming; arbitration is not. However, both parties must be willing to cooperate. Responsible businesses eager to solve problems and gain customer confidence are taking part in arbitration with good results.

At the federal level, the Federal Trade Commission maintains 11 field offices and the central office in Washington, D.C. (see Chapter 10 for listing). The Office of Consumer Affairs (see Chapter 10) is another federal agency that will either try to help you directly or will refer your problem—with comment—to another federal, state or local agency.

At the state level you may contact the central state consumer protection agency which is usually connected with the office of the attorney general. If you live in a large city, there is probably a city consumer protection agency, and most likely your county has one as well.

Not every state has a Small Claims Court, but if yours does you may wish to take your complaint there. Each court establishes its own procedures and adheres to its own standard of excellence. Some states operate very satisfactory Small Claims Court systems, while others fall far short. You may represent yourelf in Small Claims Court, so there is no need to worry about lawyers' fees, but you will have to pay a modest court fee. If you obtain a favorable ruling, this fee may be included in the sum awarded you. The amounts that can be awarded by a Small Claims Court vary from court to court.

Unfortunately, courts are not really geared to monitor the marketplace and any complainant going to Small Claims Court is likely to be confronted with delays and time wasted in waiting. Also, many unhappy consumers are quickly intimidated by the prospect of taking on a large company in a courtroom.

Although consumer action newspaper columns, radio and television shows can handle only a few of the many requests they receive, they can be very effective in those they do tackle. In the same way, community organizations have no legal authority to bring to bear on an unscrupulous dealer, but the bad publicity and general hullabaloo may be enough to win you your cause.

TEN

Who Can You Turn To?

Where can you go for information? for arbitration? for legal action? Following is a list of trade associations, consumer protection offices, and government agencies that may be of help to you. Most of them are discussed in the chapters of this book (see Index). These sources operate on a national level. There are, however, many local consumer protection groups; and a local source may be your best bet. State, county, city or independent consumer agencies that work on the local level are most aware of the conditions, pressures, laws, and sources of authority in their own specific areas. Check your telephone directory for a listing of such groups or contact your state attorney general's office for guidance.

American Society of Interior Designers
730 Fifth Ave.
New York, N. Y. 10019

Better Business Bureau (There are well over 100 across the country— check your local directory for the one nearest you. The Council of Better Business Bureaus is located at 845 Third Ave., New York, N. Y. 10022.)

Bureau of Consumer Protection (*See* Federal Trade Commission)

Carpet and Rug Industry Consumer Action Panel
Box 1568
Dalton, Georgia 30720

Carpet and Rug Institute
P. O. Box 2048
Dalton, Georgia 30720

Chamber of Commerce
1615 H Street, N. W.
Washington, D. C. 20062

Consumer Product Safety Commission
7315 Wisconsin Ave., N. W.
Bethesda, Maryland 20014

Direct Selling Association
1730 M Street, N. W.
Washington, D. C. 20036
> (Member companies of this trade association are in the business of door-to-door selling.)

Federal Trade Commission (includes Bureau of Consumer Protection)
Pennsylvania Ave. at Sixth St. N. W.
Washington, D. C. 20580
> (There are 11 FTC field offices located in: Los Angeles, California; San Francisco, California; Atlanta, Georgia; Chicago, Illinois; New Orleans, Louisiana; Boston, Massachusetts; Kansas City, Missouri; New York, New York; Cleveland, Ohio; Falls Church, Virginia; Seattle, Washington.)

Fine Hardwoods Association
666 Lake Shore Dr.
Chicago, Illinois 60611

Furniture Industry Consumer Advisory Panel
P. O. Box 951
High Point, North Carolina 27261
> (Sponsored by Southern Furniture Manufacturer's Association.)

Home Furnishings Daily
Fairchild Publications
7 East 12th St.
New York, New York 10003

Interior Design Society
Merchandise Mart
Chicago, Illinois 60654

Lamp and Shade Institute of America
15 East 26th St.
New York, New York 10010

National Association of Bedding Manufacturers
1150 17th St., N. W.
Suite 200
Washington, D. C. 20036

National Association of Furniture Manufacturers
840 Connecticut Ave.
Washington, D. C. 10015

National Home Furnishings Association
Merchandise Mart
Chicago, Illinois 60654
    (NHFA is a trade association of home furnishings retailers.)

National Retail Merchants Association
100 West 31st St.
New York, New York 10001

Office of Consumer Affairs
New Executive Office Building
17th and H Street, N. W.
Washington, D. C. 20506

Retail Floorcovering Institute
Merchandise Mart
Chicago, Illinois 60654

Society of the Plastics Industry, Inc.
250 Park Ave.
New York, New York 10017

Southern Furniture Manufacturers Association
P. O. Box 951
High Point, North Carolina 27261

United States Department of Commerce
Washington, D. C. 20230

Index